04

04.04.04

Matt King OBE

Scratching Shed Publishing Ltd

To those who have faced the toughest battles
and darkest of times.

And for those who will in the future.

Contents

Acknowledgements

OVER the past two years, as the vision to write this book became a reality, I met Phil Caplan, my editor, only once. Yet, in that time he came to know every fibre in my body and event in my life that made me the person I am. Thank you, Phil, for your guidance and for bringing this dream to life.

It is impossible to list all of those who helped me to overcome every challenge, crisis and self-doubt since that fateful day, 04.04.04. Family and friends, both past and present, without you I would not have made it through. I hope my refusal to be beaten by the constraints of disability, and the success with which I have been fortunate enough to rebuild my life will be accepted as my personal way of saying thank you.

Since its inception, the Rugby Football League Benevolent Fund has grown into the much-needed resource it always needed to be. All profits from the sale of this book will be donated to the Fund and I hope the time it has taken to write it is proof enough of my appreciation. It is now time to help others.

To my parents, Chris and Glenda, and brothers, Andrew and Michael, we have experienced the darkest of times, but made it through. Your love and support made the difference.

And Ilona-Roza, I look forward to sharing with you every moment to come on this path of ours.

Matt King

July 2015

'If you are going through hell, keep going...'
– *Winston Churchill*

Foreword
Sir Alex Ferguson CBE

I WAS asked to write this foreword through a mutual friend, that great horse racing legend and philanthropist Jack Berry.

At first I was a bit reluctant, but along with his letter was a rugby league book, *13 Inspirations*, and Matt's outline story was in there.

I must admit, I am a disciple to people who challenge adversity and turn it into an asset. Reading all about Matt's incredible journey over the past 10 years, I not only instantly warmed to him but became completely in awe of his ability to overcome such a serious injury.

One of the great lessons in Matt's story is that if you have a determination in your make-up and you value your life, then a lot of things are possible. He also has the capacity in his nature to accept help and he rightly acknowledged that from his parents, his nurses and his friends.

04.04.04

Matt confronted all the issues as he lay fighting for his life and the one thing that kept gnawing at him was the desire to live and do the best he could with his condition.

He summed it up pretty well when he realised that the negatives were not as important as the positives; he set about readjusting his future to things that were not only a challenge but that he enjoyed.

Come on, what is the guy like?

Completing marathons ... painting with a brush in his mouth ... studying law ... he sought out the value of his life and he succeeded.

In football, I've seen managers who needed to win but went conservative in their team selection and drew.

Matt persistently talks about positives. He was not going to let himself down thinking 'if only.'

This is an inspiration and from time to time we thrive on the examples of the Matt Kings of this world. They make it so easy to use their determination, to an extent that next time I have man flu, I'm going to say 'Matt King' and get on with my day.

Well done son and get on with your next challenge. There is nothing you can't succeed at!

Sir Alex Ferguson CBE, July 2015

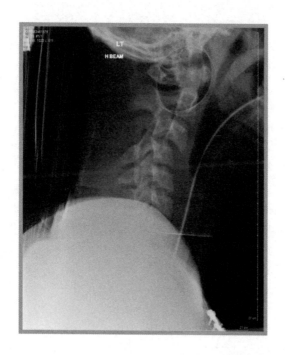

04.04.04

1.

Death Wish

I WAS in a state of utter ignorance about the vital pieces of equipment keeping me alive and had no understanding as to how they worked. Denial was a sanctuary that kept me from having to think about such things and I was comfortable in it. But laying on the bed, watching the *Six O'Clock News*, something wasn't right.

Given I had no understanding as to what 'right' meant, I couldn't put my finger on it. But I knew I wasn't getting enough air and there was a raspy sound coming from my tracheostomy site whenever my ventilator was pumping air into my lungs.

A piercing, intermittent alarm began emanating from the ventilator on the stand to the left of my bed. A shrill, undeniably urgent alarm. In a gut-wrenchingly awful repeat of the events weeks earlier, my attempts at calling for help were met with nothing. No sound.

04.04.04

I was on mute, no-one seeing the fear in my eyes as I scanned left and right looking for any signs of people coming to help, but hearing nothing. Each pump was met by a blockage, preventing the air getting any further than the end of my tracheostomy pipe to my lungs which were already beginning to crave the oxygen I was being deprived of.

The strange sound I had identified seconds earlier was air hitting a solid wall of mucus, and being sent in the opposite direction away from my lungs, and out of my body, the ventilator's alarm screaming to all and sundry with each failed attempt.

My vision was suddenly filled with three nurses frantically checking for signs of the cause of the noise. Whilst there was fear in my mind, it was manageable. Manageable because I knew that in just a few seconds, they would have diagnosed the source of my breathing problems.

But my oxygen levels were now dropping to a dangerously low level; the saturation monitor measuring the percentage of it getting through alarming incessantly, making it plain to everyone that I was on an increasingly slippery slope. There were hurried discussions across my bed between the nurses. I was now in a full state of panic.

To hear one of them say, 'I don't know what to do,' chilled me to the core. Terrifyingly, this was mirrored by the others.

With each passing second, the oxygen in my bloodstream was becoming scarcer. I was once again heading towards that black world of unconsciousness which I had hoped with every ounce of my being I would never again experience.

The nurses were checking for any obvious cause of the blockage. This, though, was not a calm, methodical

18

search, it was more in desperate hope than expectation. As I scanned their faces, I was met with looks of confusion and fear. I was suffocating, and there was nothing I, nor those around me, could do about it.

I was not prepared to give in though, despite being a seeming passenger on a captain-less ship heading out of control, but with an inevitable destination. Death.

My vision was failing me, my hearing becoming unclear, just a blur of sound reflecting the chaos around me. The downward path I had not even contemplated minutes earlier had now led me to the brink of unconsciousness, and I fell from my world into one of darkness.

Unlike my other experiences of this desolate state, I remained aware of my thoughts – and my fear. I hadn't slipped into the previously safe world of ignorance of my predicament but, rather, remained alert to the alarms outside the bottomless void I was falling into.

The fear is something totally un-relatable, so completely terrible and hideous that mere words cannot describe it.

I was desperate, my eyes scanning the darkness enveloping me for any chink of light. The darkness was not just black, it was an indescribably black blackness. It was complete; indefinite, infinite in scale, the pressure it was inflicting upon my soul was overbearing.

It was pushing down on me, crushing me and I could see no beginning nor end.

I know I am dead, but please don't let this be death. Please don't let this be what death is like, for the rest of eternity.

I was so unbelievably aware and terrified that I had died.

But it wasn't the ending of my life which I was

fighting, it was the recognition that death was this infinite, pitch-black, lonely, crushing void.

I was resigned to my fate ... to death ... though still conscious of voices, sounds, alarms and intrusions into my body; the physical efforts being made by those who were trying to save me.

But I now just wanted to be left.

Please stop, please stop this.

I could no longer bear this experience, nor the knowledge of the repeatedly awful series of events that had inflicted my being in the preceding days, weeks and months.

I had fought off as many battles as my body could take, both physically and mentally, and was at last ready to let my head drop beneath the surface of the water.

This time, for good.

2.
The Eve

ALL the talk leading up to the last day of the school term before the Easter holidays was of the eagerly anticipated re-match between Biggleswade Town U16s and their counterparts from Sandy.

Whilst the football match was undoubtedly one lure to get a rowdy group of mid-teenagers out of their homes on a Friday night, the offer of cheap booze and a 'quality' disco at which to party into the early hours of the morning sealed the deal for many.

Arriving at the ground slightly late, the party was already in full swing and, by the look of the copious empty beer glasses on the floor, there was a relaxed attitude being employed with regards to under-age drinking.

I headed to the bar safe in the knowledge that I would get served and, therefore, indulged in the luxury of arming myself with two full pints of lager and, to make it fully worthwhile, a bottle of Smirnoff Ice. I was nothing if not a classy operator.

I polished off the first beer before I had even left the clubhouse and, within minutes, could already feel the four per cent alcohol content flooding my system; on nights like these, having such a low threshold was, indeed, a positive.

I was already well on my way to being tipsy and headed out to enjoy the second half with my schoolmates but my recollection of the evening becomes more blurred as the hours passed. Whilst I would like to blame the timeframe that has elapsed since then, I would have been in no better position the next morning to explain the events of that evening than I am today, and that can be put down to my inability to say no to drink.

I assume that, for many, the night descended into carnage. There was certainly plenty of 'courting' going on, although more akin to the gypsy tradition of 'grabbing', with drunk male teenagers trying all in their power to impress the opposite sex and remain upstanding.

For me, although I liked to think I was lucky with the ladies, I wasn't. I didn't even try my luck, not through lack of desire, but rather because I knew I would get knocked back.

At school I had a pretty large group of friends or, more accurately, acquaintances with whom I would spend hours playing football, larking about in class and having a good time. But once the bell went signalling the end of the day, I would retreat to the village of Langford.

Social life outside school centred around a core group of friends, Jon, Matt, Ben and Will, but this was not their scene and whilst I mingled and got along with most of those there, I never felt confident enough to truly get stuck into the activities of the night.

The evening ended with me being completely paralytic and on a meandering three-mile walk home.

With alcohol still flowing through my system, my 7:30am alarm could not have been more unwelcome. Nor could the prospect of heading into work hungover, in need of sleep, and hungry, which at least was sorted thanks to a ham and Flamin' Hot 'Monster Munch' sandwich, courtesy of Rocket Ron, the butcher from across the road.

That combination worked nearly every time.

The morning at work was fairly uneventful, as dreary as the banter between myself and the two other mechanics Dan and Stan, both of whom had also been out experiencing the delights that Bedfordshire had to offer the previous evening.

I helped to service a 10-year-old Ford Mondeo, attending to customers wanting fuel and looking forward to my first truly competitive match for the London Broncos Academy the following day.

One o'clock came and, having shut up shop, I walked home to get my things ready for the game. To this day, I don't know why I walked as I usually used my bike to get everywhere, but I can distinctly recall walking up the driveway to the back gate, admiring my car, and generally being at peace with the world.

I was met by my younger brother playing with his remote-control car in the back garden, and having shown him my skills, left him to it and headed upstairs for a shower.

I had already prepared my kit earlier in the week and so I just needed to get enough together for the overnight stay in Halifax. I was perturbed to read that we would need to bring our own sleeping bags, foam floor mat and other bits and pieces I hadn't anticipated when reading in the fixture list a few weeks prior that we would be going up the night before.

I had visions of a four-star hotel, complimentary room service and such luxuries as befitted up-and-coming professional rugby players. In hindsight, I had massive delusions of grandeur and boy was I in for a shock later that day.

So, with rugby stuff, sleeping bag and other camping gear in tow, Dad gave me a lift to Milton Keynes coach station, as was the norm for my rugby trips up North. I arrived to be met by Stevie Elms, a precocious young talent with a mouth to match his skills.

Aside from Biggleswade and Bedfordshire in rugby union, Stevie and I also played for London Broncos through the age groups and were in the Scholarship programme from our early teens onwards. Given that he played winger and I centre, we built quite a close bond, both on the pitch and off it.

For some reason, most likely a lift, Stevie had brought his 'girlfriend', in the loosest sense of the word, to the station to see him off; sitting in the cafe, we had a pretty awkward half an hour or so waiting for the coach to arrive, mainly because she didn't have two words to say for herself.

Awkward conversation and silences were punctuated by watching her eat the fry-up he'd bought her as recompense for his absence, and I was relieved when our transport arrived. It was actually a rental van, already filled to the rafters with coaches, players and tackle bags even before Stevie and I sought to bundle on-board.

Since morning, the weather had deteriorated significantly, going from a dull day to one of torrential rain. It was dark, cold and the M1 was at a standstill for much of a truly horrendous journey. I sat next to John Sullivan, 'Sully' as I had always known him, and although it was cramped, we certainly didn't have the worst of it.

Those at the back of the van had to make do with sitting among the tackle bags that were stuffed into every available crevice. Although not best pleased about it, they did make the most of a bad situation by turning them into fairly comfortable looking mattresses and, as a reward, were the only ones able to get some sleep to pass the hours.

The van became more steamed up and stuffy and was a pretty grim place to be; the increasingly rancid air filled with the usual teenage banter mainly consisting of supposed sexual exploits and conquests, ridiculous games of truth or dare and listening to, invariably crap, music being played on the tape player.

Claustrophobia and an increasing headache, combined with the nerves which were already building in my stomach, made the relief all the more tangible when we stopped for a break, fresh air and a KFC at Keele Services.

Despite the rain, I decided to go for a walk to clear my head and just be alone for a few minutes. This helped, but you can imagine what a mix of 15 teenagers, several grown men and an equal number of buckets of chicken made of the atmosphere inside the van for the final leg.

Thankfully, we only had an hour or so before we entered Halifax, pulled up alongside a deserted grey stadium and jumped outside into the ever-increasing deluge of rain.

The Shay, Halifax's home stadium which was at the time undergoing extensive renovations and upgrades, was to me as a 17-year-old quite a formidable location at which to play my first Academy match. The nerves truly started to kick in as I unloaded kit from the van and stood in the rain amidst the Yorkshire hills.

04.04.04

Walking towards the stadium, I still had no idea what to expect. We had not been told where we were staying and given that the place was deserted, there were more than a few confused gazes exchanged between us all.

Eventually, having headed off to track someone down, our coach, Phil Jones returned accompanied by a club official and we followed them both through the ticket turnstiles into the ground, behind the North stand, and arrived at the clubhouse.

I thought we must be going to wait inside whilst our accommodation was sorted, but I was wrong. 'If you'd like to follow me, I'll show you through to where you will be sleeping,' came the response from the official and the penny dropped. It dawned on me we would be sleeping on the floor of the clubhouse. No room service. No en-suite bathrooms. Nothing but the prospect of an uncomfortable night sleep.

We headed through the door and although the bar was well-appointed, we were warned it was off-limits. There was an immediate power struggle for the best sleeping positions, with the biggest and most intimidating in the squad bagging the raised platform in the corner nearest the radiators and the water dispenser.

I was left with a sliver of floor space in the middle of the bar area, propped up against a pillar, with my head positioned next to the feet of two of my teammates on either side of me. To complete my mood, I then set about laying out my 10-year-old sleeping bag which I was relying on to keep me warm. Unfortunately, I'd had it since my days in the scouts and it was very much the worse for wear.

It had holes in it, the occasional cigarette burn and only came up to my chest. I already knew the night was going to be a test of my endurance. Whilst many of the others sat around listening to music, I did my best to get my head down.

Sleep was hard to come by, both because of my nerves, but more so the unfamiliar environment and stone cold floor. I had brought along my brand new Walkman, a birthday present from my parents a couple of weeks earlier, but given that everybody was listening to drum 'n' bass and garage, I felt slightly unsure about blaring out my Robbie Williams album, and eventually thought better of it.

My night was, therefore, spent tossing and turning, squashed into a sleeping bag designed for an eight-year-old, waiting for first light. For some reason, there were no functioning toilets in the clubhouse at that time, and I remember braving the cold, rain and darkness to negotiate the public ones in the stand.

I was only wearing my boxers and, in hindsight, it would have been sensible to take the time to put on a pair of shoes. I didn't and upon entering the toilet immediately regretted the decision. Struggling through pitch darkness and approaching the urinal, I felt the unpleasant sensation of liquid between my toes, and it wasn't rain coming in.

I went back to bed stinking of piss, with a rather unwelcome sticky sensation on the soles of my feet.

3.

The Kings

MY formative years were spent in a pretty standard semi-detached, four-bedroom house on the outskirts of Biggleswade, Bedfordshire. Ours was the last one in a cul-de-sac and at the end was Jubilee Park; a recreation ground with a slide, set of swings, one goalpost in the middle, and a bin. That was it.

Many of my earliest, happiest memories were spent at that park. I met my best friend growing up, James, at the age of nine on the swings, and played many an hour there with a rugby ball, time on my hands and endless room to practise.

My rugby life had begun at seven years old during a stay with my gran and grandad when, in an attempt to keep me entertained, grandad pulled a rugby ball from the shed and passed it to me. That was where my sporting journey began; the following weekend I went down to Biggleswade Rugby Club and was hooked.

04.04.04

I used to love playing rugby with dad. It usually involved him sending me to the park half an hour before he intended to come out, telling me to do my stretches and warm-ups while he had another brew. We would then pass and kick the ball back and forth for hours on end, just trying to improve my skills.

With rugby beginning to take a pivotal role in my life, elder brother Andrew and I started going to watch Bedford Blues when I was 11 and he 14, they were the nearest club to play a decent standard. When we were old enough, mum and dad would allow us to travel to Goldington Road on our own by bus, and that very quickly became our Saturday afternoon retreat of choice. It remains mine to this day.

They would give us enough money to cover the return fare but after just a few trips we discovered the 'Hot Shop' where you could buy pretty much any cooked meat, in any form. Before long we were doing our best to save as much as we could to splash out on barbecue ribs and chicken wings on the way to the ground.

Occasionally, we'd each buy a single ticket to a destination well before our final stop and then hide on board for the remainder of the journey. In order to avoid detection and suspicion, we thought it best if we left the bus separately. Once, as it approached the outskirts of Bedford town centre, Andrew sneaked off near an estate, leaving me massively exposed as the only person remaining on the top deck.

Sitting at the back of the bus I couldn't outsmart the driver's mirrors and when the bus came to a violent stop just after Andrew had got off, I knew my game was up. I heard the driver's cabin door open, followed by footsteps on the stairs.

'What do you think you're doing?' he shouted. 'What

do you mean?' I replied in a high pitched voice with tears welling up in my eyes.

I was marched downstairs and then forced to suffer a humiliating 60 seconds or so in front of the passengers on the ground floor, before being forced to pay the difference in fare between Biggleswade and Bedford and summarily ejected.

There I was, hungry and alone, stuck in an estate I didn't know how to get out of, with barely 45 minutes before kick-off. My brother eventually found me wandering aimlessly and near-terrified and found it all highly amusing.

Andrew and I would head to Goldington Road in all conditions. During the club's one and only stint in the Premiership, a temporary stand was erected along the length of the pitch to accommodate all the extra spectators attracted by the higher level of opposition.

Sitting in the uncovered edifice one February, during a fixture with London Irish, it was teeming down and we were like drowned rats. I don't recall how or why, but dad was sitting in the corporate hospitality boxes overlooking the pitch. With a glass of wine in one hand, accompanying canapés and a general smugness, he made sure to wave at our sodden bodies from his covered vantage point and raise a glass at our predicament. That seemed to amuse him highly.

Although dad was always strict and very quick to hand out discipline, mainly in the form of groundings or cutting the plug off the various electrical appliances in my bedroom, he was – and remains – pretty immature.

I remember one time, on the way back home after it had been snowing, we both thought it would be a good idea to see how much snow he could clip with the wing of his Vauxhall Carlton. Driving down the country roads, this went well for the first couple of attempts but, inevitably, on the third he caught a bit too much of the drift, digging the front-end of the car into the bank and then sliding sideways down the road on the verge of tipping onto the roof.

Despite being a scary experience for us both, I think we were more worried about how we would explain it to mum.

My parents didn't stop working when their sons were born, they simply split the responsibilities and roles as evenly as possible. Mum worked nightshifts as a nurse at Lister Hospital, Stevenage, for many years and, following that, was a district nurse in Hitchin.

Her car boot was always full of every imaginable bandage and dressing. Whenever I was poorly and not at school, because I couldn't stay at home, I travelled around in the car with her while she visited her patients. Listening to the daytime consumer shows on local BBC radio, I'm pretty sure I learned more from them than I ever did in a day in school.

She probably wouldn't disagree, but her corned beef hash was simply the worst. She made it in a pressure cooker, which seemed odd and it was hideous. Even now I can barely stomach a corned beef and Branston pickle sandwich, the thought of those meals still make me shudder.

Mum was a strict disciplinarian, never shy to hand out a smack to the bum if I overstepped the mark, and, I'm sure, prided herself on the clarity of the hand imprint on the cheek. It was a traditional and effective punishment.

Friday night was cleaning night and I used to dread coming home from school to what I knew would be a fraught evening.

Although my only task was simply to tidy my bedroom, there was always a clear tension as I walked through the door to be met by a wall of polish and stale musty air being pumped out by the Hoover.

Growing up I went through phases with my bedroom, either being dedicated to ensuring it was the cleanest and most organised it could be, or simply not caring. A personal best was leaving my lunchbox in the bottom drawer following the final day of summer term in year six where it remained for a good six weeks, slowly getting more rancid and mouldy. I was a pretty rank child.

Aside from cleaning night, the rattle of the ironing board opening was also terrifying and signalled my trying to stay out of the way until getting delegated the task of putting the clothes away. It never helped that we didn't have enough coat hangers but I got around this by taking the clothes upstairs and putting the ones I couldn't find homes for straight back into the washing basket. I think that showed initiative.

Mum and dad always endeavoured to keep our evening meal a family affair around the dining table, and would give us the task of tidying up the kitchen afterwards. I always hated hoovering, so would go for clearing the sides and loading the dishwasher.

When I was very young, I saw the dishwasher powder as similar to the Refreshers sweets I liked so much and proceeded to pour out a teaspoonful and eat it. Given its hugely acidic and toxic nature, it was not particularly good for my tongue, lips and stomach. It wasn't the first or last time we were grateful mum was medically trained.

With dad working long hours in London for a shop fitting firm, I would go to mum for everything. In middle school, just before my teens, it was all the rage for boys to have subtle blonde streaks in their hair. After pestering her for a long while, she finally relented and, having seen how it was done on television, insisted on doing it herself.

She thought it necessary to brace herself with a few stiff gin and tonics to calm her nerves before starting my transformation. It wasn't a good idea. The amount of tinfoil she used for each streak meant that the dye spread across my head. I knew it had not been successful when she could no longer stop herself from laughing.

As she washed the dye out, the full scale of the disaster became apparent. Big circular blotches of ginger left me looking akin to a leopard and I was stuck with this truly horrendous look – as my school friends never stopped reminding me – for a good six months before it grew out.

Dad was not conventional in the same way as mum when it came to administering punishment. I remember once, when I was about seven or eight, returning home from the park with him and desperately needing a pee.

For some reason, I decided I couldn't wait the 10 seconds for dad to open the door and went in the front garden. He caught me and, understandably, went spare. Following the initial bollocking, he sat me in the front of his car and took me to a local quarry.

Stopping outside the giant iron gates which had a sign on saying, 'No Entry. Trespassers Will Be Prosecuted. Danger! High Voltage', he told me that this was the entry to the naughty boys home and that if I ever did anything like that again he would be dropping me off and never returning. It had the desired effect of terrifying me into complete submission.

Dad was always one for attention for detail and it extended to the shine on my school shoes. Every Sunday evening, I was banished to the garage with a tub of shoe polish, a brush to apply it and another one to take it off. I would remain there until I could see my face in the reflection and would go into school every Monday morning with a shine resembling that of the Queen's Guard.

But for all this, his childish streak was never far below the surface. He would find it hilarious to wake me up by rubbing a cold flannel directly onto my face and take equal pleasure in watching me jump from my slumbers.

There were three years between Andrew and me, and although he was someone I looked up to, he was also there to fight with – constantly. You couldn't call our relationship close, we never really spoke unless it was to argue and I took great pleasure in winding him up. To this day, Andrew's proudest moment is dropping me on my head whilst I was still in hospital just after being born. As a result, he credits himself for the many flaws in my personality.

Given the age difference, whenever we fought I would always lose. Andrew had both the size and brain to beat me quite easily. He also knew how to inflict maximum pain with minimum effort, being particularly adept at nipple cripples, Chinese burns and dead legs.

However, one thing we did see eye to eye on was sport. With homework finished, most evenings and weekends you would find us kicking a ball down the park.

When I started both lower and middle school, Andrew would always be entering his final year there. Being his younger brother certainly gave me a certain kudos with the older students, which invariably saved me from getting my football kicked far away by them at lunchtimes.

At middle school, we would exchange a cursory nod when we would see each other in the corridor but other than that would stay out of each other's way. That seemed to work pretty well and, as we got older, we certainly stopped arguing as much.

By the time I reached upper school, Andrew was in year 12. Although we maintained a brotherly indifference, the added advantage was that he could start driving. Andrew, in his ultimate wisdom, bought an E-reg Vauxhall Nova in bright red, kitted out in designer mats and car seat covers from Halfords. In hindsight, that probably wasn't a great look, but it did give him a greater pull with the girls as it put him in the minority of boys in the school with a car. More importantly, it gave me a lift to school.

Younger brother Michael is, and has always been, monumentally big. At the age of three, he was probably the size of the average teenager. I was always jealous that he was more popular with Andrew's friends who nicknamed him 'Schmick', after the legendary Manchester United goalkeeper Peter Schmeichel.

As a baby, I'm fairly sure he didn't like me. When he was about two, I had been asked to watch him in the living room whilst mum made the dinner. I sat him on the couch and, much like I did most evenings, settled down to watch *The Simpsons*. Immediately he started crying, but as I picked him up to stop him disturbing my viewing, he clamped down with his newly-attained teeth on my index finger. It was extremely painful – my first memory of Michael is one of hurt.

Although there was a bigger age difference between me and him, and we too fought, I usually got the upper hand, which may have something to do with why I felt closer to Michael than I did to Andrew.

Michael was always getting into mischief and I vividly remember mum and I saving his life. For some reason he thought it was wise to climb into the wardrobe; he could only have been three or four years old at the time.

The next thing we heard was a biblical crash from upstairs, where we ran to find the wardrobe lying flat on the floor and Michael nowhere to be seen. Only his screams were audible.

I guess it was the adrenaline but despite being only eight-years-old, I managed to lift the wardrobe whilst mum extracted her youngest from his temporary tomb. He was understandably terrified and she furious.

Growing up, whenever I would have a nightmare, I would always head for Michael's bed and sleep with him. Embarrassingly, this probably lasted until my mid-teens and it never filled me with pride to be comforted by someone five years my junior.

Michael is very much happy-go-lucky and at school was a bit of a terror. We could not have been more different in this respect. He was always getting into trouble and, on one occasion, in his ultimate wisdom, Michael thought it wise to put his finger through the flies of his trousers and pretend it was his penis. Doing this in front of a classroom of 13-year-old girls did not go down well, however, and he was hauled up in front of the police accused of indecent exposure.

In my formative years, we spent most of our holidays in the South of France. We visited resorts all down the West coast and invariably stayed in a mobile home on one of the Keycamp campsites. I used to love the feeling of loading up the car on the evening before we left; opening suitcases which still had sand in from the previous year, the smell of sun cream and preparing our bikes signalled the start of the holiday for me.

Every time we would take them, strapped onto the

roof and the bike rack at the back of the car, five in all, together with ten suitcases and other assorted paraphernalia that severely tested the rear suspension.

On one occasion, we were due to sail from Dover at 6.45am and, somehow, against all their instincts, mum and dad slept through the alarm and only woke up at 4.30. Chaos ensued and we must have averaged over 100mph down to Dover, which was exhilarating for the boy passengers if not the fraught parents, but we made the ferry just in time.

Once in France, the long journey in the middle of summer was horrible with Andrew, Michael and myself crammed into the back of the car. It would have been uncomfortable if we were small, but with all of us having taken dad's tall genes, it was a hideously hot, sweaty journey.

Arriving at the campsite, the trip quickly deteriorated into chaos when Michael thought it would be a good idea to pull the indicator stalk off of the dashboard. Because my one and only job whilst mum and dad unpacked the car was to look after him, clearly it was my fault.

Having enjoyed a peaceful two weeks in the sun, sea and sand, on the return journey we left the campsite at five in the morning for a mid-afternoon crossing from Calais. We had only gone about 10 miles, it was dark and we were driving through forest, when suddenly there was the most almighty bang. I had been asleep but was rudely awoken as a wild boar had run into the road and hit us head on.

At 50mph, it made a mess of the front of the car and the animal. Not wanting to get out in the dark and face an irate boar with a headache, even to assess the damage, dad drove on regardless until we reached the next town to decide what to do next.

The front end of the car was pretty much destroyed

but it was driveable, albeit with bits of pig hanging off. Every stop we made on the way north was the chance for me to inspect the carnage and, as a 10-year-old boy, it was very exciting and I became quite obsessed.

Breaking up our annual pilgrimage to the South of France, the following year we went to Cyprus in what was my first experience of flying.

Having explored all that the island had to offer, I wanted to go home with something to remember the holiday by, to show off to my friends that I'd been somewhere far away, and to impress the girls.

I thought a necklace would make me look cool so opted for that, but having searched many shops in the local area without success, on our final day in Larnaca, I was losing hope and everyone else patience.

I spotted a stylish boutique that looked like it had the right sort of trinket. I went in and found the perfect piece, a rope necktie with a ying and yang-type metal centrepiece. I think it cost three or four Cypriot pounds which was equivalent to a couple sterling. Having spent a good while in the shop choosing, the rest of the family came in to inspect the purchase and, as we were walking out, I was behind my mum and brothers.

Dad was following me and as I stepped through the door, I clipped one of the tiered shelves housing some of the expensive glass and ceramic ornaments in the window display. It came out of its housing and fell onto the one below, which in turn crashed onto the shelf further down, which then cascaded onto the one underneath it.

You can imagine the scene. Glass everywhere, shattered ornaments, porcelain heads detached from porcelain bodies. And, in amongst all the mess, price tags –

and expensive ones at that. There must have been hundreds of pounds worth of damage.

Mum heard the crash and returned to see the carnage and destruction. With the manager apparently out the back, the shop assistant ran over but she was very young.

Dad tried to negotiate but she spoke very little English. Focusing on the fact that the shelf was apparently not properly secured, he offered her 15 Cypriot pounds in damages, everything he had in his wallet.

The shop assistant knew it was wholly inadequate but couldn't go to get the manager for help for fear that we would leg it. Rather than accept the money, dad forced it into her hand and said that was all she was getting before sternly commanding me to walk.

We went calmly down the High Street until we got to the first corner, turned it and ran. We didn't know where but didn't stop until we were well clear of the disaster area. The only problem then was that we didn't know where the car was and the long search began in silence as we surreptitiously retraced our steps to find it.

As soon as we got to the car, the inevitable earful ensued. However, I think my parents understood how upset I was – my hysterical crying gave them an idea – and they soon let up on me, realising it was an accident. By the time we got back to the hotel, they were almost sympathising with and comforting me, but my brothers took great delight in my suffering and milked it for all it was worth for the rest of the holiday.

On one of the occasions in France, I had my first romance. I must have been 12 or 13, and on the second day at the campsite, Andrew, Michael and I met up with some other English kids and were playing football on the five-aside pitches. Watching was the most beautiful girl with blonde hair, a gorgeous face and massive boobs, it was the ideal combination and I was both mesmerised and somewhat intimidated.

I never spoke to her, thinking she was out of my league but, much to my surprise, she approached me one day when I was laying by the swimming pool. Her name was Hannah and she was from Sheffield. How very exotic I thought.

We spent much of the next few days together, frolicking in the water, spending time at the beach and in the evenings as part of a bigger group of kids. But on the final night before she was due to leave – desperately, three days before me – Hannah and I kissed, the first proper one I had ever experienced and I'm sure I briefly touched her boob.

This is a huge moment in any boy's life and made my holiday. However, the next day, after she had left, my world fell apart. The remainder of it was spent crying in the mobile home. My heart was broken.

4.

Pre-match

THE most profound, life changing day started fairly ordinarily. I hadn't been able to get my head down for too many hours during the night and I woke in Halifax with a mixture of tiredness, nerves but also intense adrenaline.

Travelling up the day before had started the whole pre-match preparation a good 24 hours earlier than I had ever experienced and, irrespective of what I did to take my mind off it, there was always that undercurrent of apprehension in the back of my mind.

On a dull, leaden day in West Yorkshire, I wanted nothing more than to be out there on the pitch and for the game to begin.

Early, before showers and breakfast, a pitch inspection had been carried out at The Shay, and given the almost constant deluge of rain that had fallen over the previous 24 hours, it was decided that the pitch would not stand up to two matches in a day, and so our curtain-raiser to the first team clash was cancelled and relocated.

That was a massive anti-climax. I'd been looking forward to making my debut on such an historic surface since being selected.

Disappointed, I packed up my sleeping bag and everything else I wouldn't be needing for the day, and headed out, with the rest of my teammates, to get washed and dressed on the other side of the stadium.

The changing rooms, and dribbling, cold showers were a pretty grim affair, a tight squeeze to say the least and not the ideal preparation to kick-off the day.

We were then issued with our kit. It wasn't what could be described as a formal shirt presentation ceremony, but rather Phil Jones came around to each squad member in turn, handed them their jersey, and everyone just continued getting on with their own business.

I would be starting at right centre and would wear squad number 17 for the season befitting my junior status in the squad, and the fact that I would have to fight for a starting berth.

I spent a good 10 minutes strapping my ankle, and once all the squad were ready in their match kit and tracksuits, we headed out together to grab breakfast in the stadium restaurant. As we left the changing room, the Halifax Academy squad were sitting in the North Stand and there were more than a few glances and stares exchanged as each player mentally profiled their opposition.

As I entered the restaurant, I was delighted to be hit by the smell of a full English being prepared and settled in to making the most of it. Saying that, aside from the nerves and the adrenaline pumping through my system, I had a pretty bad stomach, and so wasn't able to polish off as much as I would have liked.

My memories of that meal are so incredibly vivid, and I distinctly recall that the sausages were amazing, and I complemented them with bacon, scrambled eggs, mushrooms, baked beans and a couple of slices of toast.

I had to dash off halfway through as my stomach ache was getting worse but it was the last breakfast I would ever eat under my own steam, and it was a good one.

Meal completed, stomach emptied and Red Bull drunk, we headed out to the van to be told we were going to nearby Savile Park, where we would complete our warm-up before moving on to the pitch on which we were to play.

The day had by now brightened up with sunshine attempting to break through the cloud cover, and although the wind still had a kick to it, conditions were pretty much perfect.

By the time we arrived, every window in the van was open in an attempt to avoid suffocation through Deep Heat inhalation and we were pretty pumped to get going.

Having been for a quick jog and completed our stretches, we started with some ball skills and contact drills, something I had done thousands of times before and came as second nature. They were the most basic, standard exercises, not designed to test skill or ability, but rather just get the body ready for what was to come.

But not that day. Standing in line to receive a pass from Sully, my feelings of unease were overwhelming. I couldn't focus and in the 20 minutes that followed, I made numerous uncharacteristic mistakes. I'm certain that if one of the coaches had picked up on it, I wouldn't have started the match.

Kicks I would normally catch were dropped. Tackles I would normally complete were clumsy. Passes were inaccurate. I simply put this down to my worse than usual nerves and was sure the errors would pass as soon as the game kicked off.

Everybody was pumped. The start of the season we had been training and preparing for over the previous months was minutes away and the competitive edge in every member of the playing and coaching squad was evident and intense.

In my mind, I was going over the team plays we had been working on for the past weeks and envisaging my initial tackle, as I did before every match. I was ready.

Back in the van to go to the match venue, I don't remember whether we got lost, but it seemed to take an age to reach the ground.

I was again sitting next to Sully, in the window seat, and was scanning the passing scenery for glimpses of rugby posts or pitches. I couldn't see any and as we turned into a residential street, lined on both sides by houses and trees, I was sure we were going the wrong way.

Almost without warning, the van pulled up to a stop alongside the pavement. Looking out to my right, I could see the entrance to a housing estate, but just further ahead, a low stone wall beyond which looked to be a playing field.

As always, my gumshield was tucked inside my socks, and I decided to leave my tracksuit on until the last possible minute; that was always something my dad had instilled in me, and had always stood me in good stead.

The opposition were already well into their noisy preparations and had taken occupation of the nearest end of the pitch, but I had more important things on my mind; the litre or so of water and Red Bull I had drunk in the previous couple of hours had caught up on me, and I was desperately seeking for a spot to take a pee.

Failing to find an appropriately shady spot, I decided that up against the brick wall around the circumference of the pitch was as good a place as any. Once finished, I trotted past the Halifax squad and their supporters and joined up with my teammates just before we headed into our traditional pre-match huddle.

Huddles are a ritual familiar to all team sports and I had been either involved with or led them since the age of seven, when starting out in my first season of touch rugby. This one was different though.

Never before had I experienced the intensity of ambition and desire as I saw in the face of our captain, Louie McCarthy-Scarsbrook. It was enforced upon every member of the squad, through the emotion in his words, with each player drawing from them what they needed. They weren't poetic, but they did the job.

We broke from the huddle and crossed onto the pitch to take our positions. As we did so, Stevie and I exchanged a brief hug, and headed across to the far right-hand side of the field.

At the coin-toss, handshakes were exchanged between the captains as I glimpsed at my opposite number. Seconds later, having won the toss, Louie elected to kick-off.

The ball on its kicking tee and having confirmed with both captains that they were ready, the referee blew the whistle. It was struck high and long into the arms of the Halifax half back, positioned 10 metres from his own try line on the opposite side of the pitch to me.

As I ran forward, I remember consciously thinking to

myself that I had taken my first step along the path towards professional rugby that I had dreamt of all my life.

The half back shipped the ball on to one of his props who was met by Louie and Sully in what was a sickening crash of bodies. It was a huge hit but, to his credit, their player made good metres, causing our defensive line to retreat.

The action was still on the far side of the field, so I was able to identify the most likely attacking threats. As their dummy-half prepared to play the ball, our defensive structure came into play with every player barking out our calls in unison; 'Ready'…'Ready'…'Hit'…

Again, there was a fierce collision, halting their onrushing player before he was able to make too much ground. I found myself standing on the 40 metre line just inside the opposition half.

5.

Growing Up

MY first school was Lawnside and when Mrs Clark taught me to tell the time in year three, I thought I was a big boy. I also kissed Hayley Collins.

I'm pretty sure that got me the lead role of Prince Charming – who else – to her Cinderella in the Christmas play that year.

I loved the festive season as a youngster. Whilst from about the age of seven I was beginning to become aware of the huge sham that was Santa Claus, I still liked to convince myself that there was some truth in the flying reindeer, huge palace at the North Pole, and the overweight man slipping down the chimney.

But it was never the religious significance that gave me butterflies in my stomach, more the far more serious business of receiving presents.

Every Monday, I went to the Jupiter Cubs, I can still

recite the mantra. Never one to get the badges, that was probably a good thing as I certainly wasn't one to sew them on. In my three year stint, I amassed a total of eight, six of which were eventually attached to my uniform.

We certainly weren't a pack for football, our team was terrible and I faced the weekly humiliation of losing to my school friends in other teams. I can't say I added anything other than aggression and we never won a single game.

We went on camp to Boyd Field and, fuelled by a ton of sweets we'd spent all our pocket money on, my best mate James Garton and I thought it would be a good idea to shake the tents in the middle of the night, pretending there was a hurricane.

Marched outside in our Y-fronts while the damage was inspected, on viewing it the next morning, the metal poles were almost bent double and subsequently useless.

My real passion around that time was cycling, which I did mainly with James. We were always quite competitive and spent hours on our bikes, riding everywhere.

During our summer holidays, we would often cycle the three miles to Sandy Hills, where there's a large RSPB nature reserve. We'd make a picnic and spend whole days there.

Once we'd struggled to the top of the hill, we'd turn around and let gravity do the rest. That was immense fun, as we could reach some truly dangerous speed and would have to dodge tree roots, other cyclists and walkers in our path.

Inevitably, that also led to some huge crashes. On many occasions, James and I would return home bloodied, crying, with our clothes ripped, and the bikes in a bad state of disrepair.

Evenings tended to be spent having marathon races

around the track we made on Jubilee Park which encompassed the slide, the swing and the bin and meant some outrageous crashes. Often, to spice things up further, we would pee on the corner at the end of the slide to make it more slippery.

I frequently had to return home at the end of the night and put my clothes straight in the washing machine without telling mum. I'm not sure the terrain there has ever really recovered.

My bike was a Raleigh Activator and when I came home I invariably took it into our garage and gave it a wash down, talking to it and thanking it for surviving the race. I loved that bike and was devastated when I wrote it off.

I was 11, and during the summer holidays was racing with my friends around a racetrack we had made in the cul-de-sac. Running fourth or fifth behind James, I couldn't really see what was coming. Disastrously, as we were heading down the alleyway behind my house, my front wheel went down an uncovered drain and I was thrown headfirst into a wall.

The impact was so severe it split the outside of my *Teenage Mutant Ninja Turtles* crash helmet down the middle. My bike followed me into the wall, the impact forcing the plastic brake handle in half, turning it into an improvised spike, which embedded itself in my arm when the bike hit me.

Running home screaming to mum, it had left a hole so deep that the fat layer was weeping out – there wasn't much blood, but it was a very impressive wound which I showed off when playing football with my brother later that day.

My Raleigh Activator was no more. As a replacement,

04.04.04

Santa Claus brought me an envied Raleigh Max, with bullhorns, a speedometer and massive wheels. That gave me the edge I needed over James and I started winning.

Unfortunately, on the notorious 'piss' corner during one of our battles, our handlebars interlinked, causing a monumental crash. I was thrown forward, but rather than going over the top of the handlebars, my scrotum struck the upright.

The pain was excruciating but what was worse was pulling down my pants, and seeing blood leaking from my ballbag. To James, it was hilarious, whilst my only obvious course of action was to run home and show mum.

Trying to maintain her professional cool in the face of my hurt and embarrassment, all she could do was laugh and I stormed off to tend to my wound myself. The following day, every kid in the district had heard about what I'd done.

Graduating to scouts, my time with them did not last long. Six months in, we were celebrating St George's Day by parading through Biggleswade. There was an accompanying service in St Andrew's Church and I was sitting in the front row with James.

The songs were rather mundane and so James, myself and a couple of others decided to amuse ourselves by making up funny words, almost invariably bringing in sexual references as most teenage boys are wont to do.

We couldn't stop sniggering at our brilliance and that was noted by the Chief Scout for Bedfordshire, and also the vicar. Unbeknown to us, they submitted formal complaints about our behaviour and at the following scout session on the Thursday, all the parents were invited to attend.

There was general business to attend to but at the end they started discussing issues that had arisen with certain scouts during the highly prestigious occasion. My heart sank. 'I will be giving white envelopes to the parents of those scouts against whom complaints have been made,' said Akela and handed my father one.

Dad gracefully apologised for my behaviour and quietly left the room. I followed, sure in the belief that I was about to get the biggest bollocking of my life. Although I was right, I could never have anticipated the gravity of their anger and disappointment. I have still never seen my parents so annoyed.

I was grounded for a month and dad didn't speak to me for weeks after, my bedroom was cleaned every day and I was in bed by seven each evening. Somehow I got back into their good books but it was definitely the end of scouts.

James and I became pretty much inseparable, also being in the same class at school. We had sleepovers in his garden under canvas and embraced the challenge of sneaking through the back door, past the living room and into the dining room where the alcohol was stashed.

It was there I discovered vodka and hangovers.

James was always very much cooler than me. He seemed always to have the latest clothes, the best computer console and I was quite jealous of him. I got my first bona fide piece of labelled clothing when I was about 10 years old; granted, it was from the car boot sale, but nobody knew and I milked my Puma King blue and black T-shirt for all it was worth.

I loved that T-shirt, but it too was the victim of a crash on Sandy Hills when a tree appeared in front of me, sending me over my handlebars and tearing it down the seam. Although mum did her best to salvage it and turn it into a tank top, it was never the same.

Middle School was Edward Peake and sport became a big thing. I was goalkeeper for my year – including a highlight moment, scoring from a goal kick in the fierce derby with Holmead Middle School – and discovered cross-country running where, in year five, I reached county level.

The County Championships was a two and a half mile course but I sprinted the first hundred metres, got a stitch and ended up hobbling round and finishing 13th.

Despite playing junior club rugby by then, I only had one game at Edward Peake. Having witnessed the free-for-all it turned into, with little supervision or instruction from the teachers, my parents saw the danger and banned me.

AWAY from sport, I also dabbled with learning the tuba, an instrument the size of a small ship which sounds like a foghorn, especially when played badly. Walking to school with this Goliath of a case wasn't much good for my street credibility nor my chances with the girls, so I dropped it pretty quickly.

From Edward Peake, it was on to Stratton Upper School where I began to go off the rails.

Again sport was a centrepiece for me with football played every lunchtime in the tennis courts. What I lacked in skill, I did my best to make up for in good old-fashioned ire. Rugby had taught me that and by the end of the lunch hour, I was usually a sweaty mess.

In my first year there, it probably wasn't wise to trip up Paul Watson, who'd probably been the toughest kid at Edward Peake. Picking me up by the throat after we clashed, I was thankful that our 10-year friendship since lower school dissuaded him from inflicting anything other than a public dressing down.

In hindsight, I should have known better than to start with him as, in an art class, when we'd been drawing a live guinea pig, Paul's pencil slipped and he stabbed the poor creature.

Appearing for the school rugby team, I was one of only two people in our side to ever have played the game. Our team was pretty terrible, and only ever won one game – against Hastingsbury from Luton. Towards the end, with us winning, there was a mass brawl and I heard one of the opposition shout: 'Get the kid with the red gumshield.' I looked round to see who they meant, and realised it was me.

By year nine, I was becoming too concerned with girls and being popular. Often I'd sit at the back trying to show off to the likes of Sarah Wade and Katie Venning, two of the big shots who'd come from Gamlingay, but that quickly changed when Miss Harper moved me to the front in geography to ensure I was made an example of.

It was the most important intervention of my schooldays. I had no choice but to work hard and immediately began to get great grades. The better they got, the more confident I became and that saw me through to the end of school.

The only blip was in English literature in year 10. In the end of year exams, everyone's grades were read out and when it got to A*, mine was the only one left. I smugly thought they were saving the best until last until I was asked to stay behind to speak to the teacher, Ms Morgan.

I'd got an F which shouldn't have come as a surprise as I hadn't read the books. That put an end to my complacency and for the next year I worked my damnedest to get the best grades possible in my GCSEs. It worked and later that year I passed my exams with flying colours.

I was desperate to have the freedom to do what I wanted with my friends, and that required money. Every Friday evening after school I would play snooker with Jon, Matt, Ben and Will, but in truth, I was by far the worst. Aside from my wayward aim, having bought a bowed snooker cue from a car boot sale didn't help.

I GREW up knowing the value of hard work. Andrew began a paper round delivering the *Bedfordshire on Sunday* to some of the less salubrious areas of Biggleswade when he was 14, and somehow, the whole family got roped in.

We'd all get up early to put leaflets in the paper and then he and I split the round using wooden trolleys. Mine wasn't easy to manoeuvre especially when trying to get away from a notorious Rottweiller in Winston Crescent which used to rip the paper from my hands and shred it in front of me as I turned and ran.

I got my own round aged 13 when we moved to Langford and did it on my bike. I actually quite enjoyed it because I loved being outside whatever the weather and seeing the sun rise. It was a good start to the day, getting the blood pumping.

I was paid a meagre £12.50 per week for six mornings' work so, in order to boost my income, every Christmas, I would deliver cards to the houses signed 'Your paperboy, Matt x'. That got me about another 70 quid.

But little of it was spent on booze. Mum and dad had always encouraged me to drink when at home so that they could regulate the effect and keep an eye on me. However, the tactic failed at Clare Bowpitt's one Saturday night.

I arrived after watching the Blues and could see I had some catching up to do and duly began to drink everything offered to me. As the evening moved into night, the party was getting more outrageous and raucous as word spread throughout Biggleswade and more people kept arriving.

It was therefore no surprise when the police turned up. Given that I was 15 like most of the others and not too keen on getting caught, I ran. The house was in the middle of an estate and the maze of streets, combined with my drunken condition, soon had me lost.

Somehow, I managed to call dad and incoherently asked him to pick me up and he found me draped over a road sign on the outskirts of town. All he was worried about was me being sick on the seat of his car.

As soon as I got home, I was forced to drink two pints of water, stick my fingers down my throat and be sick into a bucket in the back garden. I woke up the next morning with my first true hangover and feeling very sorry for myself, but it was rugby training.

Dad thought it only fair to tell the coaches of my drunken state and request that they pay particular attention to my fitness and attentiveness during the session. I was sick and slept for the rest of the day, lesson duly learned.

In my endless pursuit for money, I harassed pretty much the only viable business in the village, Langford Service Garage, for a part time job cleaning the shop once a week. It was for two hours every Thursday afternoon at a fiver an hour.

Despite playing rugby at every available opportunity, I had got rather portly and had a pretty substantial stomach on me, possibly because I was giving most of the wage back to the garage shop on sweets.

I enjoyed cleaning the shop, as much for the company of Dan and Stan, the two apprentices, as the money. I liked spending time around them, listening to their banter and conquests, although I had no idea what they were talking about for most of the time; sex, drugs and rock 'n' roll were all very new to me.

Occasionally I helped stock and serve in the shop and, when it came to the cleaning, I was pretty meticulous. After a couple of years, I guess my thoroughness – enhanced by neat handwriting – had endeared me to owners Russ and Linda and they offered me the job of filling out the MOT certificates in the official logbook.

That took my tally up to £12.50 for the paper round, £10 for cleaning the shop, and £10 for the MOT and it got even better when I received a phone call during spring half term in year 10 asking if I was free to come into the garage to help out as Stan was off sick.

I jumped at the chance and it became a more permanent role during school holidays and every Saturday morning. I did very basic tasks such as short services, cleaning brakes and changing tyres, but I loved getting my hands dirty and coming home with oil all over my face.

Spending Saturday mornings in the garage, listening to Jonathan Ross on Radio Two and eating ham and Flamin' Hot 'Monster Munch' sandwiches was a great way to start my weekend. And when I had finally grown a few inches and sprouted hair in all the right places, I joined Dan and Stan for a few drinks after work in the local.

After my GCSEs, I enrolled with two job agencies in Biggleswade, looking for any work possible.

After a couple of weeks, they got in touch saying they had a job for me at Jordans Mill where they make cereals, cereal bars and all things breakfast related.

The hours were 6am to 6pm, with an hour for lunch

and a 15 minute break mid-morning and one in the afternoon and when combined with constant manual labour it was a pretty tough shift. I was stationed at the end of conveyor belt. The cereal was filled into bags and then they were put into cereal boxes which, in turn, were packed into large cardboard boxes.

Once they were full, my job was to lift them to a waiting pallet. It was tedious and pretty intense but at the end of my second week, I caught a break. I was asked if I wanted to go and work up in the fridge where all the fruit was stored in huge vats before being passed along vibrating conveyor belts where it dropped into the cereal and was mixed in.

There was very little supervision and all I had to do was make sure there was a constant flow of fruit which basically involved shoving my hand in and pushing it along. However, I had it on pretty good authority that it was a perk of the job that you could stuff your face with as much fruit and nuts as you liked. I felt sick as a dog when leaving work most nights.

In the run-up to my 17th birthday, I had saved enough cash to get myself a new car. I searched all the internet websites, bought *Auto Trader* and convinced myself I could get myself a bit of a looker: alloys, tinted windows, nice body.

In the end I accepted an offer from Russell at Langford Garage to take an E-reg Peugeot 205 in white, with hubcaps, dreadful bodywork, a pretty rancid interior and the engine the size of a lawnmower. It was a steal at £450.

Despite dad's downright refusal to teach me to drive, he did relent and took me to an unused strip of concrete near to our house where he showed me the basics. I really wasn't very good, I kept stalling and managed to hit the one pile of dirt and rubbish as I was attempting a reverse, three-point turn.

I spent hours inside the car cleaning it and one day, when that was done, thought I would give a hill start a go on our driveway, as it had a 15-degree upward gradient.

My first attempt saw the car stall and roll back a little, towards the road. That happened a second time, and a third, and by now I was in danger of getting stuck, the rear end blocking the high street through the village and no-one at home to help me.

Thankfully, my fourth attempt was successful and I inched my way forward to my parking spot, got out, and vowed never to attempt it again until I was proficient.

For my birthday that March, mum and dad bought me 10 driving lessons, which I was due to begin a couple of weeks later after I had returned from the week-long school trip to Belgium.

I never did start them or drive the car again.

6.

Life Changes

HOW I would effect the first tackle was something I envisaged before every match and exactly the scenario I had played over in my mind earlier in the day.

This was it, my first involvement as a London Broncos Academy player, my first step on the ladder I hoped would lead to a career as a professional rugby player – how good did that sound?

'Ready' ... 'Ready' ... 'Hit', came the call. From my standing start, I moved forward, flanked by teammates. The ball went from dummy half to an on-rushing forward. Here was my target.

As he caught the ball, he set off hard and low, gathering pace, the ball tucked under his right arm. It was immediately clear he wasn't planning to sidestep me, or attempt an off-load. There would be a collision.

I targeted his waist with my left shoulder. Planted my

feet. Dipped to lower my centre of gravity. Threw my body into the tackle just as I had been taught and done thousands of times before… Nothing.

Nothing. As I tried to regain my senses, there was nothing. No feeling. No movement. No sound. No pain. Nothing.

I was lying on my back, my eyes scanning everything for a sign of help, but seeing nothing. An unbelievable pressure was building up in my neck.

As a reflex, I turned my head to find my teammates, and felt something pop in my neck. There was an instant feeling of release, then there was nothing.

Looking up, my vision was blocked by a player wearing blue and white. Black hair. Terror in his eyes. 'Are you alright mate?' he part-shouted, his voice rising in apparent panic.

My immediate instinct, matched by every fibre in my body, was to scream 'HELP!' Only I couldn't speak.

No sound came from my lips. 'HELP ME'. 'HELP'. Inescapable, uncontrollable, unimaginable terror flooded my senses. More faces appeared, the absolute fear in my body reflected in their eyes.

Hands braced the side of my head. More and more bodies surrounded me. 'What have I done?' were the only words I could muster.

But I knew. I knew it in the depths of my soul, and I knew it in their faces. Pressure continued to build in my neck. It wasn't painful. It was a dull, ever-increasing blackness of pressure, with no beginning or end. It was just there. Blackness. Constant. Everything lost focus.

'Stay calm, you are going to be fine…'

'Concentrate on your breathing, slow it down…'

'Matt, look at me. Focus on my eyes. Matt. Milton. Calm down, help is coming.'

Nothing. I shut off. I stopped thinking. The frantic activity around me just a blur. Seconds passed. Minutes passed.

There was yellow. The yellow of high visibility jackets. Lots of yellow. Blue synthetic gloves. A silver thermal insulating sheet. Noise. Constant words.

'Matthew, you're going to be fine. Move your toes for me.' Nothing.

'Matthew, wiggle your toes for me please.' Nothing.

In this cocoon of panic, I *was* moving my toes. I was doing everything asked of me. Moving my toes as I had for the first 17 years and 15 days of my life.

'Matthew, this is really important. Please move your toes for me.'

Voices continued around me.

'Can you see any movement?'

'No, nothing. Ask him again.'

Reality was sinking in. I couldn't move. I couldn't feel. There was nothing of my body left. Amidst the terror flooding my mind, the horrendous dots began to join.

'Matthew, I am touching your wrist. Which wrist am I touching?'

Nobody was touching my wrist.

'I don't know. I don't know. I can't feel you...' were all I could scream at the top of my non-existent, breathless voice.

I couldn't get any air.

Fighting for oxygen brought me back, focused on this hellish nightmare at the centre of which I was laying. I couldn't breathe. 'I can't breathe. HELP'.

04.04.04

No sound escaped my lips. Looking up into the eyes scanning down on me from the person bracing my neck, he couldn't compute what I was saying. 'I can't breathe. I can't breathe. I can't breathe.' No sound.

With every attempt to scream, the panic rose within me, air escaped my lungs, and I was drowning. I could feel my life slipping away.

A broken neck. Paralysis. Life in a wheelchair. No life at all. A broken neck.

It was all I could think.

As I could feel the oxygen escaping my body and the blackness enveloping me, I was overcome with a feeling of calm. There was no longer fear, panic or terror. I was accepting of the situation and aware that these were my last breaths on Earth.

There were no last words professing love for my family, just resignation to my fate and thoughts of mum, dad, Andrew and Michael. No specific thoughts, they were just there with me.

'Matthew, stay with me! Stay with me! Look in my eyes… Don't give in!'

'Matthew… Matt, stay with me. Milton, you're going to be fine…'

It was too late. I could feel life slipping from me, I'd given it my best.

'Let me die' were the last words that didn't escape my mouth.

There is unremitting darkness.

7.

A Contender

IT was on a Friday evening after school, while playing pool with Jon, Matt, Will and Ben, that I received the phone call I had been waiting on for days.

Having trialled for the London Broncos Academy weeks earlier, the club's head of youth performance, Phil Jones, rang to confirm my place in the squad for the season.

Putting the phone down, I could not have been more elated to share the news of my position on the first rung of a professional ladder I had dreamt of climbing all my life.

The seeds had been sown a decade previously during my first visit to Biggleswade Rugby Club when, in the heat of summer, I arrived hiding behind dad's back and ceremoniously burst into tears.

With Andrew also playing, rugby turned into the focus around which our family's weekends tended to be centred.

04.04.04

My preparations would start the evening before as dad made it clear that if I wasn't ready, I would not be playing. I would cram my boots, socks, shorts and shirt into my kitbag, making sure to never forget my gum shield, without which he would not let me walk onto the pitch.

The first season was huge fun but on top of learning the basics of the game I also had to come to terms with being given a new name, 'Milton'.

There were three Matthews in the squad, and with the full version and Matt already having been taken, my initials MK, and our proximity to Milton Keynes, determined how I would be known.

From that day forward, I was Milton to my teammates. I was even Milton to my dad in everyday life.

During that season in the U8s, although our kit was navy blue throughout, I wore a pair of white shorts. The team was always coordinated in every photo, the image of solidarity – apart from me.

I loved playing when the weather conditions were at their worst; rain, wind, snow and mud were ideal for throwing myself into it and coming off the pitch looking unrecognisable. When I got home, dad would make me stand outside in the garden in my boxers, and hose both me and my kit down, something he always seemed to take perverse pleasure in.

I couldn't see the sense in washing my kit just to wear it again a few days later, so it stayed in my kitbag until the next session.

That allowed the smell of sweat, blood and Deep Heat to mature into a quite disgusting aroma and every week, without success, I regretted it and vowed not to do it again.

My first coach, Geoff Stillwell, remained with the

team until we were U11. Playing in the County Cup that year, we had reached the final which was played at Leighton Buzzard. With children and parents everywhere, the club officials took to protecting the first-team pitch by cordoning off its perimeter with rope.

With excitement and adrenaline fuelling me, I ran as fast as I could from the clubhouse to where my teammates were warming up. I simply did not see rope blocking my path and, having been erected at waist level for the adults, it was perfectly aligned with my neck, lifting me off my feet and throwing me to the ground.

Like a scalded cat, I bounced up off the floor and with blood oozing from my neck, ran screaming to where my parents and teammates were waiting. I was attended to by St John's Ambulance as the boys went on to win the cup, my only memento a scar which spanned the width of my neck.

As a team growing up through the age groups we were hugely successful, going entire seasons without losing a match and, at 15, led by our coaches Paul Raitt, Pete Biernis and Ivan Couchman, we were named by *Rugby World* magazine as the number one team in our age group in the UK.

That year, as a true test of our credentials, we entered the most prestigious national tournament available to us, the final of which was to be a curtain-raiser to the England versus Barbarians match at Twickenham in May 2001.

With our reputation preceding us, we arrived in Nottingham with a point to prove and, with the eyes of the opposition on us, our preparations weren't exactly typical. During our warm-up for the first match, rather than making lots of noise to intimidate them, as they were doing, we gathered on the halfway line to do the hokey-cokey.

04.04.04

I was slightly self-conscious as I belted out the lyrics, 'you put your left leg in...', but with everyone else throwing themselves into it, it worked; we must have unnerved them. Not only did we overrun Droitwich, we made our way to the final.

The six-week period between the tournament in Nottingham and the decider at Twickenham was hugely intense. Training three times per week, coaches and specialists from other clubs were brought in to give us the added one per-cent it was hoped would make the difference.

Playing at English rugby union's spiritual home is something very few get to experience and even aged 15, I appreciated that. Every aspect of my life was focused on that 30-minute match.

The big day came, and our bus set off from the rugby club at 7am. As much as we were encouraged to get our heads down and relax, I couldn't.

The stadium was a quarter-full as the match kicked off, 20,000 people looking on, but it was the hundreds who had made the journey from Biggleswade who eventually calmed me. With their singing, banners and encouragement, that was all I needed to go out and do myself justice.

Bournemouth were our opposition, we had two disallowed tries and dominated territory and possession, yet the match remained scoreless until partway through the second half.

The pivotal moment came when we were awarded a penalty midway inside their half.

Richard 'Chard' Plenty placed the ball on the tee, before going through his ritualistic routine and stepping forward to kick the goal.

Towards the posts it went, and as the cheers went up

from the crowds, I automatically raised my hands in celebration; only to see the ball pass across the face of the posts before being caught by their full back.

The game ended in a draw and although not the ideal way to resolve a match, the referee tossed a coin to decide the winner; heads was called by us, and heads it was. We had won, as unsatisfactory as it was.

As we were escorted from the pitch, I knelt down and picked a handful of the hallowed Twickenham turf. I wanted a permanent reminder of the day.

Waking up the next morning I felt an uncontrollable sense of loss. Everything which my life had revolved around for the previous two months was over, there was a void. I remember laying on the sofa in the front room with a pillow over my face just crying.

From the age of 13 onwards, I had been selected to be part of the Bedfordshire Youth County set-up, and so alongside playing at Biggleswade, for six months of the season I would play against counties from the South of England and Wales.

Given the rather peculiar rate at which I grew, my position for both Biggleswade and Bedfordshire chopped and changed significantly. In my younger years, I was always one of the taller players and spent the majority of my time at fly half or centre.

But, having hit 12 years old, I stopped growing almost overnight. I stayed the same height for years whilst my teammates, and opposition players, continued their spurt. As they grew upwards, I grew outwards, and by the time I hit 15, I was rather rotund.

Given my cannonball shape, I was moved from playing in the backs to the front row. Apparently this would give the team mobility but in reality I knew it was just because I was now too slow to play anywhere else.

I wasn't used to being involved in the general physicality of the forwards and it came as a shock to the system. There was a massive learning curve, given the need to understand scrummaging, lineout work, and throw myself into every ruck, maul and tackle.

But I knew deep down that I was no longer athletic enough and had no choice but to embrace the move and do my best to oust the Biggleswade and county hooker, Duncan Couchman.

It turned out to be a fairly successful transition, so much so that by the end of the season, Duncan and I were sharing the load for club and Bedfordshire.

Simultaneously, my rugby career was taking another direction. Aged 12, I had been playing in the local derby between Bedford and Biggleswade at the home ground of Bedford Blues, Goldington Road.

We lost narrowly, but in the Bedford ranks was young superstar Matt Cook whose father, Les, had played rugby league for Oldham and had strong links to that sport in London.

Les approached my dad in the clubhouse to ask whether I would be interested in playing rugby league for the newly formed Bedford Swifts' juniors.

With the added prospect of trialling for the London Broncos Scholarship Programme a possibility, I jumped at the chance.

Having played only three or four matches for the Swifts, I soon found myself travelling down to London to train with the Broncos juniors.

That invariably entailed going north every second

Saturday to play one of the other Super League junior sides in Yorkshire and Lancashire.

I was quickly drafted into the London Broncos Scholarship Programme and benefited from more regular training sessions in the capital, access to the Broncos' first team support staff, such as physiotherapists, and received greater input in terms of nutrition and diet.

For three consecutive seasons, I was also selected to represent the South of England and Wales in a number of regional tournaments against Yorkshire, Lancashire and Cumbria, although the pool to choose from was not extensive.

Heading up the M1 for the games, I could not help but feel that, as mainly recent union converts, we were out of our depth.

There were a number of embarrassing scorelines where we were totally outplayed but against Cumbria we were more than a match, winning two of our encounters and losing one.

By the time I hit 15, I was playing club and county rugby union and representative rugby league, and given that my GCSEs were fast approaching, something had to give. I simply couldn't commit the time needed to train and play as well as working towards my exams and so took the decision to drop playing league.

I still wasn't getting as much enjoyment from the game as I should have been and whereas I had previously set my heart on playing professionally, I was now more realistic and understood that I should focus my attentions elsewhere.

Dropping league gave me the freedom to do more things I thought important, and I was soon taking on the extra roles at Langford Garage, seeing more of my friends socially and, in August 2003, preparing to tour Australia and New Zealand with the Bedfordshire Tigers, a team led by Ivan Couchman and cherrypicked from the best players from East Midlands.

It was a once in a lifetime experience but cost £3,000. My weekly work savings were supplemented by a substantial compensation payout I received following a rather one-sided fight with Alex, whilst in year eight at school.

Having stood up for Emlyn, one of my friends, following a nasty challenge in football at lunchtime, Alex turned on me, leaving me with a broken nose, two chipped teeth, and dented pride.

Following the police investigation, it turned out Alex, an African immigrant, was two years older than he had claimed and had questionable paperwork. I received £1,500 towards the trip.

Once it was confirmed that I was going, I soon set about saving. I had a metal tin on a shelf above my bed which contained all things important to me; money, aftershave and photos. I created a spreadsheet, it was all very professional, and set myself deadlines by which time I needed to have accrued the required amount.

At our first training gathering, all the players and coaches agreed a set of ethics and morals for both on and off the field.

Dignity, respect and professionalism were very much at the heart of the values and they were evident in everything we sought to achieve.

Our aim was to travel to the other side of the world and represent England with pride which very much appealed to me, and from that first, tough, fitness-centred training session onwards, I was counting down the days to the trip.

I had never been away on my own before and with my new Antler suitcase packed, I sat down with mum and dad to receive a lecture on what I needed to be careful about.

Although I would never have admitted it, I was pretty scared, not only about what was to come over the next month, but also about leaving them for so long.

And, for some reason, I also decided to make a statement and travel with dyed bright red hair.

Our first match in New Zealand was against Christchurch Boys High School, the cream of rugby-centred establishments there. It turned into a fractious, backs-to-the-wall effort and a narrow win. We had two players sin-binned, the game was abandoned early and then made the national press over there and back at home.

We then defeated Wellington District in an absolute mud bath and won narrowly again in Auckland, where we played Papatoetoe. As 16-year-olds, we thought something was up when their massive players drove themselves into the car park, some of them carrying children. It turned out they were U21s.

Highlights of the first part of the tour were white water rafting on the Kaituna River, throwing myself off a waterfall and a bungee jump at Taupo into the Waikato River.

With a 150-foot leap off a cliff face into the waters below, I had absolutely no intention of doing it but, with mounting excitement as I watched and peer group pressure, I gave in and agreed.

As soon as I leapt, a sense of freedom and exhilaration seemed to overcome me. The five seconds it took to hit the water seemed to pass in slow motion and I don't remember experiencing any fear. It was really quite a feeling and I was thrilled to do it while I had the chance.

04.04.04

Arriving in Melbourne, I was immediately struck by the cosmopolitan nature of the city. I truly fell in love and, where possible, did my best to explore it, taking in a game of Aussie Rules football at the Melbourne Cricket Ground, walking the Formula One track and visiting my first strip club.

We stayed there for four days during which time we played Melbourne Harlequins, beating them comprehensively.

In Sydney, we defeated Eastern Suburbs in a game that was punctuated with fights. The following day, the GCSE results were out. With my parents on holiday in Crete, it was left to Andrew to pick up my results from school.

Given that we were 10 hours ahead in Sydney, his attempts to contact my mobile were in vain; in all, I had 11 missed calls and seven voicemail messages, each with a noticeable increasing anger in his voice.

I rang him back to receive the terse news that I'd got three A*s, four As and three Bs. I was relieved and pleased in equal measure, and could now relax and enjoy the rest of the tour.

On our final day in Brisbane we played renowned side Sunnybank. It was an evening match and so we spent the majority of the day at 'Wet 'n' Wild', the city's largest waterpark. Whilst fantastic, it wasn't ideal preparation for the challenge that lay ahead of us that evening. Playing utterly exhausted and with a sunburnt back, by half-time we were losing 32-0.

We dominated after a half-time bollocking but were unable to claw back the deficit and suffered our only defeat on tour.

The climax, and the moment I had been anticipating most, came in Cairns; diving the Great Barrier Reef.

Though first there was a game against Brothers, played in incredible humidity with the weariness of the schedule kicking in.

I gave away an intercept try early but got it back with one of my own in a match of increasing tension. Coming away as healthy winners, the animosity continued after the final whistle when a further fight broke out in the tunnel and Ivan had to take the opposition coach aside to dampen the atmosphere.

It was not how we would have liked the final match in Australia to end.

Having qualified as an open water scuba diver a couple of years previously during a family holiday to Malta, I had the necessary qualifications to allow me to dive independently.

It was a beautiful day as the catamaran set off but I spent the entire, wave-crashing hour out to it with my head hanging over the side of the boat being sick into one of the greatest natural wonders of the world; not something of which I am too proud.

Having watched a number of documentaries in the run-up to the trip, I had a fair understanding of what to expect but nothing could prepare me for the tranquillity and beauty, it was by far and away the most magical experience of my time in Australia.

The trip had truly been a life-changer.

My time off from playing rugby league allowed me to concentrate my focus on Biggleswade, Bedfordshire, and potentially East Midlands.

And the growth spurt I longed for finally arrived approaching my 16th birthday – being well worth the wait.

Within six months, I had lost all my puppy fat, was

scaling six foot and was too tall to play in the front row any longer.

By the time the first match of the U16 season came round, I had nailed down the fly half spot with Biggleswade and was loving playing the game again.

I trialled for the East Midlands U18 squad against players one or two years older, but that motivated me. I did everything I could to be vocal, domineering and confident in all facets and played well all weekend. At the final whistle of the selection match, I knew I had made it.

I was proud to be one of only four players of our age selected for the squad, and when returning to Biggleswade for training and matches, I was able to walk a little bit taller.

As part of the U18 regional tournament, we played six regions from across the South. East Midlands, at this age group, had been unbeaten for the three previous seasons, and so there was huge pressure upon us to uphold the honour.

We won our first five matches by fairly clear margins, and in the decider played Nottinghamshire, Lincolnshire and Derby, who had also won all of their games. It was a shoot-out that we just claimed 33-31.

All season I had played second fiddle to Pete Vickers, who went on to represent England in an U18 tournament at the end of the season and whilst I knew I would have a second crack the following year, it was nevertheless disappointing.

Having completed my time with East Midlands in mid-December, it was during the two-week Christmas break from school that I received an invitation from my former coach at London Broncos, Phil Jones, to trial for their U18 Academy side.

I expressed my doubts as to whether I was good

enough, or indeed if I even wanted to get involved again, but Phil said all the right things and the following week I arrived at Brunel University with the rest of the trialists.

The two-day process was designed as the final stage of selection before the squad was announced, and was completed with a full-length match between a team of certainties and those on the fringe.

I was in the fringe squad and whilst our team was over-powered, I out-played my opposite number. It was the following Friday that I received the phone call.

Training with the Broncos was incredibly intense. Our fitness coach, 'Oggy', took it to an entirely professional footing, with bespoke conditioning and nutritional programmes for each player depending upon their size and position.

For the first time in my life, I was regularly lifting weights, taking protein supplements and really looking after myself.

For the first two months of pre-season we concentrated on fitness, team plays and gelling as teammates. But as soon as the fixture list was released everyone became focused on 4 April, the date of our first league match, away to Halifax.

8.

Reality Hits

SOMETHING terrible, utterly unthinkable has happened. A feeling of dread and unease fills every cell of my body. Is this me, or am I looking in on the life of somebody else?

Time has no meaning.

Hazy semi-consciousness replaces the black curtain enveloping my physical and mental state. The truth of the situation slowly begins to dawn, like water entering the cracks of a rock. This isn't a dream.

This is my body, my mind, my life, at the centre of this unimaginably bleak, terrifying and incomprehensible reality; total uncertainty and fear mixed with the concoction of medication that is inevitably controlling my awareness.

I know that something is wrong, something has changed, but my mind cannot grasp the extent of it amid this unending darkness. It is like mist permeating my fingers. Sand through a sieve.

I am not yet ready to understand my new reality, or the events bringing it to bear.

I am lying on my back, facing the ceiling, utterly restricted and unable to move. I can see no faces, but sound is again entering my world.

I hear my mum's voice. There is comfort in recognising a sound I have relied upon on almost every day of the previous 17 years and 17 days of my life.

But it also confirms the worst.

There are unfamiliar sounds of machines buzzing and alarms shrieking.

There is no pain but instead, where feeling had previously been, just a dull numbness. A heavy, oppressive force exerting itself on my physical being.

My toes. My feet. My legs. My stomach. My chest. My arms. My hands. My fingers. Something in the recesses of my mind, in the whisper of an understanding that something terrible has happened, draws the connection.

'Matthew, this is Dr Ross. I am going to ask you some questions. If you understand what I am saying, if you understand what I'm asking, I ask you to blink your eyes once...'

'Do you know who you are?'

One blink: I know the person I am.

'Do you know what your name is?'

One blink: Matthew.

'Do you know where you are?'

One blink. The subconscious understanding within me telling me that something is wrong gives me the answer. Again, panic, as my understanding of my situation creeps up on me and intensifies.

'Do you know what I am going to say to you?'

Feverish thoughts focus on the incessant terrifying images that have commanded my brain during the previous 24 hours as my body remained prone, broken and comatose.

There are blue skies. Sunshine. Grass. Yes, I was playing rugby. Blue and white shirts are running towards me. I am laying down. I cannot move. No sound will escape my lips. There are faces looking down at me. High visibility yellow jackets. There are voices. A stretcher. No air. I cannot breathe.

I have broken my neck. I will never again voluntarily move any part of my body below it. My life is fading away. I am letting it fade away. All fight has left me. Darkness.

One blink.

There is someone stroking my head. Fingers running through my hair. I know instinctively this is mum. Other than my gran, she is the only person ever to have done this to me, and it has always been a source of comfort.

Today is different though. Today, this is the only thing she can do to help me, helpless as she is. Today, this is through desperation and her attempts to comfort her son are in vain as I know in my heart, my head, and from her voice that I am at the bottom of a deep, dark, desolate well.

Mum's comforting gesture and words do nothing to alleviate the terror flooding my body. She tells me everything will be okay, that *I* am going to be okay. But I know that my life has come down a one-way street from which there is no escape.

I am faced with two alternatives, both unthinkably grotesque: either slip away into the dark void of death that I had contemplated and succumbed to on the pitch, thereby relieving my soul of the torment of a desolate future; or fight my way back to consciousness and the brutal realisation that

I will be, at best, a shell of what I once was. I am unable to talk, move or shake my head to show my mum and the doctors that I understand the grave situation and so tears just well in my eyes and overflow down my cheeks.

No words. No movements. But in those tears is the knowledge that my life on this planet, as I have lived it, enjoyed it, but ultimately taken it for granted, is over.

I close my eyes, choosing the option that will spare my soul the hardest walk along the most desolate of roads, at the end of which is no destination. Blackness once again floods my world.

FOR how long I was sedated and unconscious I cannot say, but I became aware that I was still alive when an oppressive stream of air forced its will upon me.

My body was no longer able to breathe on its own, such was the extent of the damage my dislocated third and fourth vertebra had inflicted upon my spinal cord. To continue living, my body was reliant upon oxygen being pumped into my lungs through a face mask creating an air-tight grip on my face.

It took away from my determination the choice of whether I fade away into the eternal grip of death or live to face the unimaginable fears I would inevitably encounter.

The Bipap facemask which had become my link to life was inescapably uncomfortable. The rubber seal had to be tight enough to prevent any leakage of air from the contours of my face, I was totally subservient to its vice-like grasp.

I was aware of the presence of people around my bed. Who they were and what they were saying, I could not compute, but there was an understanding that I was not alone. There were spectators at my battle with life.

But more than anything, I was aware of an indescribable pressure pinning my head to the bed from which there was absolutely no escape, no let up and which was claustrophobic in the extreme.

Unbeknown to me, 'Halo-Traction' had been applied to my skull: seven pounds of lead weights suspended from wires attached to a metal cage round my head.

Screws had been drilled into either side of my cranium, the concoction of drugs coursing through me shading my body from the worst of the pain that they were inflicting.

The weight of lead was intended to stretch my spine, easing the pressure that the dislocated vertebrae were exerting on my spinal cord.

Night cast a shadow over the intensive care ward and left me feeling an even greater sense of vulnerability and isolation. It was desperate to be so dependent upon others, and yet unable to reach out for their help.

I was trapped in a private hell.

Given the lack of air passing over my vocal chords, no words could escape my mouth, but I started doing all I could to affect the situation. Manipulating every muscle in my face to loosen the stranglehold of the mask proved fruitless, yet in that moment I did discover a way of gaining the attention of those around me.

Moving my tongue in my mouth, I realised I could make a weak clicking sound.

The relief that this realisation brought cannot be overstated as, for the first time, I was able to have an input, as insignificant and tenuous as it may have been, on the events unfolding around me. One click. Two clicks.

'Matthew, are you okay?' came the response.

04.04.04

The oxygen passing through the facemask dried my lips and mouth terribly. One click. The facemask was ever so gently lifted away and there are eyes looking down into my own.

'D…Dr…Drink,' was all I could mouth to the nurse. I was so utterly desperate to feel the simple joy which would have come with the sensation of water passing over my dry lips, tongue, and into my broken body.

But my world was shattered by the shaking of her head and accompanying, 'I'm sorry, Matthew, I can't do that,' with the facemask replaced, cocooning me again.

Soon, the nurse returned, holding a small pink sponge, attached to a cardboard stick, very much similar to that of a cotton bud, and having dipped it in water, spread the glorious liquid across my lips.

It was the first moment of comfort I'd had and brought with it a sense of calm. As soon as the first drop touched I craved more but, all too soon, the mask was replaced and I was once again alone.

During those first days in intensive care, it became clear that the Halo-Traction was not having the effect intended on the alignment of my damaged spine and so surgery was deemed the only course of action.

A cervical discectomy was performed, an operation to remove the damaged disc between my third and fourth cervical vertebrae and to fuse those bones to one another.

Metal rods and screws formed a cage around the dislocated section of my spinal column, releasing the cord and realigning my neck, replacing the one around my head. By this time, the extent of the irreparable damage to my spinal cord was apparent and it was confirmed that my body would never again breathe of its own will.

A tracheostomy was inserted into my windpipe through a hole cut in my throat, thus allowing artificial ventilation by means of a portable ventilator giving me 12 breaths of air a minute, and has done so every second since that fateful day.

Waking up with this foreign fixture in my throat is a feeling I cannot forget. At first, it was hugely uncomfortable, akin to sticking your fingers down your throat and my natural reaction to the gag mechanism was to panic, causing all hell to break loose in the intensive care unit as my pulse and blood pressure went through the roof.

But this immediate shock and fear was soon replaced by resignation to a situation which had already spiralled out of all control. Sadness overcame me and, again, tears welled up as the only form of physical grief I could express.

The damage to my spinal cord was causing all my bodily functions to fail in unison. A urethral catheter was inserted through my penis to drain my bladder of urine and I was suffering bowel accidents every few hours.

My stools were incredibly loose due to the quantity of medications and stimulants flooding my veins, and the huge self-preservation process my body was attempting.

The consequent loss of dignity underpinned much of my time in Leeds, the hospital to which I had been brought from that playing field in Halifax. I was vomiting time and again, even though my body simply had nothing left to give.

My stomach stopped working, leading to an enormous build up of gas which had nowhere to escape and a slow, but constant, bloating of my belly.

Having been moved onto Ward L6, the Neurosurgical Intensive Care Unit, I remember it was brighter because of the lights around me.

04.04.04

I was again struggling with my breathing; I had now lost all control of my chest wall muscles and was unable to cough to clear secretions and mucus laying in my lungs. It was as if I was slowly taking on water and drowning.

Every time my oxygen saturations dipped below 92 per cent, an alarm would be triggered, prompting the nurses based on the station opposite the base of my bed, to come running.

Clearing my lungs involved pushing a thin tube into them through the tracheostomy, which was attached to a suction machine.

When the tube reached the bottom of my windpipe, the nurse placed her finger over a hole in the top of it, thereby creating a vacuum and causing the mucus build up to be sucked out of my body into the machine.

Time and time again the alarm would go off, at all times of day and night, repeating this hugely violating and uncomfortable procedure.

The accumulation of mucus quickly became too much for the suction process to keep pace with, resulting in the collapse of my right lung.

Physiotherapists attended to me almost constantly, rolling me from side to side, applying chest physio with their cupped hands to create vibrations and dislodge the mucus, and saline saltwater was pumped into my lungs through my tracheostomy to moisten and break down the secretions.

My oxygen saturations were steadily reducing, each attempted suction was resulting in the minimal removal of mucus and, more than anything, given the trauma my windpipe and lungs had endured over the preceding days, my lungs and tracheostomy site were bleeding.

At every turn, my body was failing; not through lack

of strength, desire or willpower, just because I simply wasn't able to fight off each of these blows.

I was transferred onto a specialist pivoting bed which would roll me from side to side, thereby transferring the areas of pressure from my bum and back and helping prevent pressure sores.

Moving position, and allowing gravity to take effect, also began to help move the mucus. There was a noticeable sense of relief from the physiotherapist and I could sense more oxygen entering my body. Slowly but surely, I began to feel that I was no longer about to suffocate or drown.

Ward L6 was constantly alive with activity. My world was confined to a bay in which my bed faced onto the nurses station and was surrounded by a curtain. As much as I tried to shut myself off from the horrors afflicting the lives of others playing out around me, I simply could not.

Alarms. Machines. Nurses' conversations. The agonising cries of family members.

There was a young boy in the bay next to me, he must have been only four or five years old, who had suffered a traumatic injury and whose brain was swelling, causing it to be crushed within his skull.

His death was a slow but inevitable certainty and, as the trickle of family members entered the ward, their grief became not only audible but hung tangibly in the air with every second that passed.

His suffering brought home the precariousness of my situation and grasp on life and left me wanting to shut my eyes and escape even more.

If asleep, my subconscious was still programmed to the young, healthy boy I had been days earlier, but my dreams were tortured.

In all of them, I was lying on a beach with bright blue skies, the warmth of the sun on my skin, and sand between my toes, a perfect summer day.

But I was on my back, my arms and hands uncontrollable, waving up and down, much like the tail of a whale as it is propelled through the water. My hands begin rubbing my chest, and I can feel pins and needles spreading across my torso, my body is no longer mine to control.

On waking, the agonising onset of reality brought profound grief and sorrow. I could feel the actual residue of pins and needles on my chest and I clung to the hope that my body was repairing itself, that I was getting feeling and movement back. Hope, against hope.

I was on the ward for 12 days. On the wall opposite my bed was a light box on which were displayed the electronic images produced by X-rays, CT scans and MRI scans.

It was a hive of activity as doctors undertook their diagnosis and did give me some form of stimulus as I looked across and attempted to understand each image.

There were no windows on the ward and so I never had an understanding of what time of day it was. There were no clocks I could see and artificial lighting everywhere, it was constantly disconcerting.

The one constant during all of this time was the presence of my parents. As a nurse, mum had been surrounded by such horrors all of her professional career. Dad, on the other hand, had no such experience to draw on and I can only imagine how out his depth he felt. Helpless to help me. Helpless to help mum.

Some of my personal belongings were brought up by my grandparents and I had my Walkman to help me pass the hours away. That was a blessed relief and *Now 67* became my soundtrack. The first song on the CD was Britney Spears's 'Toxic'.

Both Andrew and Michael were brought up the day following my accident to potentially say goodbye to their brother. Michael was just 11 years old and too young to fully understand the severity of the situation, and a couple of days after I got hurt, my uncle and aunt took him away with them to their holiday home in Portugal to shield him from the worst.

Andrew stayed in Leeds for much of the time I was in hospital; he was 21 at the time. To this day, they have never treated me any differently by virtue of my disability and, even in these darkest hours, he continued to take the mick out of me.

Amid such oppressively grave surroundings, it was nice to be viewed normally. Andrew bought me some half decent CDs and the film *The Italian Job*, a rehashed release in 2003, which I was allowed to play on a DVD player and TV that had been hastily arranged by the ICU staff, and placed at the foot of my bed.

My level of consciousness at that time was such that it took days to finally watch it all the way through.

Following the cervical discectomy and insertion of my tracheostomy, I was allowed to eat and drink.

My body had already started redirecting my calorie stores and muscle supplies with the aim of concentrating all resources towards repairing my body. I was already losing weight and in need of all and any energy I could consume.

I craved ice cream more than anything else, even though I had absolutely no appetite, and so a tiny tub, not much larger than a petri dish, took me days to finish.

During my time in Leeds, everything was broken; my

body, my soul, my family, it was a case of looking ahead minute by minute.

The task of securing a specialist bed in a spinal rehabilitation unit was started very early on after my transfer to ICU. Whilst spinal cord injury is a relatively rare occurrence, the recovery time for each patient is very long, and so such beds are highly oversubscribed and in great demand.

Nearest to home in Bedfordshire was the Royal National Orthopaedic Hospital, Stanmore, and the National Spinal Injuries Centre, Stoke Mandeville but, despite incessant calls, time and again, the consultants in Leeds were met with negative responses.

My family were told that it could take months for such a bed to become free and the decision was taken to allow me to be nearer to them and my friends whilst my recovery continued and that the Luton and Dunstable Hospital would be my next interim home.

By this time, I had become immune to what was happening and was now resigned to the stultifying daily routine. I was a sad, lonely and scared young man.

There were a huge number of preparations that went on behind the scenes to arrange the transfer. The plan was to fly me from Leeds-Bradford International Airport down to London-Luton using an air ambulance, which was effectively a small, lightweight aircraft fitted with state-of-the-art medical equipment, piloted and manned by trained paramedics to care for me during the journey.

I wanted nothing to do with any of it. They could have my body, but not my mind. Therefore, when asked by the doctors whether I would like to stay conscious or rather be anaesthetised and sedated for the duration of the transfer, there was no decision to be made. I would close my eyes and shut myself off to the world.

There was activity all around me. Equipment being packed up. Medical notes completed, but I was lost to it. My eyes were shut. If I closed them, I could escape and find a sanctuary of deep, dark silence within my mind. My mum simultaneously stroking my head was all I needed in addition.

Suddenly, there was interruption, a softly spoken female nurse confirming it was time to go. My eyes were forced open.

Five nurses and healthcare assistants congregated around my bed to roll my horizontal prone body through 90 degrees onto my left hand side. My head was held in place by a nurse who never stopped explaining what was happening, reassuring me and asking if I was okay. I did not respond.

Once on my side, a plastic board was slid under my bed sheet to allow me to be transferred onto the trolley I would be on in the aircraft. I was returned to laying on my back, my head and neck immobilised using sponge blocks and straps, as were my limbs, to stop them becoming trapped or sliding off the board.

Once secured, my physical being was ready to take the next step on its awful journey. My inner being was not.

On the count of three, the five people slid me from my hospital bed and onto the trolley. My eyes remained shut. Closing them tight meant this wasn't happening.

'Matthew, you're going to be fine. I'm here with you. Don't worry.' Mum knew what to say and began stroking my head again.

My eyes remained shut but tears escaped from the corners.

04.04.04

A nurse said, 'Matthew, we are ready to go. You are in very safe hands. Would you like to go to sleep?' The slow, measured nod of my head was the only indication I gave.

My mum gave me one final kiss on the forehead and then she was gone, I was once again alone in this nightmare.

Suddenly, I was on a sunny beach in France with my family around me, the sand on my skin, sun on my face and blue sky up above. Sedatives flooded my system. My body was theirs to do with as they pleased; my mind was at peace.

9.

Parents' Nightmare

DESPERATELY trying to cling on to my best memories from the past, blocking out the present and not even wanting to think about the future, I was resigned to my fate. I was not sure I had the will to fight on.

Days were drifting into each other, so much was happening around me that either I wasn't aware of or just didn't want to know about.

My recollections fuse around the time of my accident as the days interminably drifted.

Having to cope with a phone call every parent would dread and the immediate implications thereafter, the lives of mine also changed irrevocably.

They are best placed to continue the story.

Dad, Chris, admits that he doesn't remember much detail about the events which unfolded after the accident, believing that he subconsciously blotted them out.

Mum, Glenda, on the other hand, being a district nurse remembers just about everything and because of her training was very aware of the medical treatment I was getting and, in her own words, was a Rottweiler in ensuring that everything was done properly and in my best interests.

Chris: I'd taken Michael over to play football in Bedford and when I got back had a phone call from Phil Jones to say that Matt had been hurt. I phoned Glenda.

Glenda: I had been really busy all morning and on my way back to the office for lunch had popped into the local supermarket. They had an offer on for Easter eggs and I put three in my basket as I got the call.

It was Chris, asking me how soon I could get home. Why? Well, Matt's been hurt. OK. He's been airlifted to hospital....Oh. I remember standing there thinking, 'I'm going to have to buy these Easter eggs or I'll have to pay for the parking'. It's funny what goes through your mind when you can't really take in what is being said to you.

I came to my senses, dropped the basket, ran out to the car and drove home. I had my uniform on and when I got changed my hands were shaking. Chris was telling me to calm down, it would all be all right.

I had to hand over all my work for the afternoon to another colleague. Chris had already Googled a map of the hospital, we knew he was going to Leeds General Infirmary and we didn't have satnav at the time. We even had to find out how to get to Leeds.

Chris: Glenda drove a Ford Puma at the time and I had a Carlton. I thought the Puma would be a lot faster in getting up there but I remember thinking, coming back, he'd be far more comfortable in the back of my car which is bigger. I always look on the bright side.

Glenda: On the way, someone from the Broncos rang telling us, 'It's OK we've sorted out a hotel for you' and I remember thinking, 'we're not going to need a hotel, we're coming to collect Matthew and bring him home.' It was actually irritating me, I just needed to speak to Matthew to know he was ok.

Chris had been told Matthew had a neck injury. We'd been at matches before when players have been airlifted to hospital with similar injuries, they always came back later, feeling very brave and congratulated by their friends and families.

All we needed was for Matthew to ring us. I remember I was holding three phones, Chris's, mine and my work one. I kept looking at them, willing one of them to ring, Matthew at the other end saying, 'Hi mum, it's me.' The call didn't come and the nearer we got to Leeds, the more I worried.

When we finally reached the hospital, Chris stopped at the entrance to A & E and I flew out of the car. He went to park while I went in. Some of the coaching staff were waiting at the entrance and took me in.

They spoke to reception, telling them who I was. I remember the receptionist saying, 'I'll go and get someone to see you now'. This wasn't good, normally you have to wait for ages before someone comes to see you in A & E.

I went to the loo thinking I don't want to come out of here. When I did, a sister was waiting for me, and she guided me into a small office. I knew by now that things were bad and I had no control over any of it. I was in the middle of a really bad nightmare, I just needed to wake up and everything would be okay.

There was a sofa on which I was sat. A doctor was in a chair opposite, leaning forwards towards me, the way you do when you are breaking bad news.

Someone gave me a glass of water but I was shaking so much I couldn't hold it and they had to take it back. The doctor said, 'Shall I tell you what has happened?' I replied, 'No, wait for Chris.' Another minute or so before I had to face what had happened.

I'd been on a communication training course at work the day before and on that they said you only remember a third of what you're told. That kept going round and round in my head, 'You need to remember everything, keep concentrating, make sure you remember everything they tell you.'

Chris came in, and sat next to me. That's when they told us: neck injury; high level; looks bad.

My head was a racing mixture of thoughts. 'Christopher Reeve. *Christopher Reeve.* Oh no, my baby, my perfect boy, this isn't happening. Matthew had everything to live for: he worked so hard, always busy, always fun, I don't think he had ever hurt anyone in his life. THIS CANT BE HAPPENING.'

They explained about the neck injury, about the swelling, about needing to wait until we knew the extent of the damage. The swelling could cause further damage. My immediate response was, 'give him steroids.' They are always given if there is swelling: only not for spinal injuries. They told me this was something they didn't use for neck injuries – they do now.

'I need to see Matthew', I kept saying, only I couldn't, he was having another scan done at the time. I just needed to see him, to hold him, to look after him, give him a hug and make it all better. They took us up to the Intensive Care Unit, to wait for him to arrive.

Chris and I hugged and held on to each other in the corridor. They were settling Matthew in his bed. He was unconscious, covered in drips, with a breathing tube in his mouth. His body was still. I could see through all that and just to him - I took no notice of the machines, I was used to it. For Chris, that must have been really hard.

I went close to Matthew and said, 'It's okay, Mum's here,' and was shocked when he shook his head, I saw the nurses glancing at each other; the knowing look between them. I said, 'You've not sedated him enough, he needs to be sedated some more'. They did that immediately and we had no further response from Matthew.

Later in the afternoon they washed him and he still had his rugby socks on and that really upset me, the tears started again.

Chris: I was frankly useless - everything was happening and I was just a passenger, I didn't contribute anything. I was just trying to support and be there for Glenda. It was worse for her because she knew and understood what was going on. I knew it was bad but I didn't really know what that meant.

Glenda: We were making phone calls all evening to people to let them know what had happened. Michael was at a birthday party. We'd already arranged for him to be picked up but we needed to get him looked after for the night. Andrew was working in Luton and didn't live at home.

We had no clothes or anything with us. One of the nurses gave us a pack with things in like a comb and toothpaste. They said they'd made arrangements for us to stay in the hospital for the night and gave us this key with a great big handle on it.

I remembered the call on the way up. I knew arrangements had been made for us to stay in a local hotel. We asked how far away it was and whether we could walk it, we were told it was five minutes so opted to stay there instead.

Before we left that evening, Matthew was quite stable. They were doing quite a lot with him and I was watching them like a hawk. When we left I said to them, 'I doubt we'll sleep tonight so if there's anything at all, please ring us'.

I cried, wailed all night long, then we got up early and went back to the hospital next morning.

What a shock. They had fitted a halo device to his head. Bolts drilled into his skull, with metal work attached to it, putting traction on his neck to stretch it. I stood still in the bay and said, 'Why didn't you ring us? Why didn't you tell us what you were going to do? I should have been with him, looking after him. Who gave you permission to do this?'

I was suddenly aware of the awkward glances and people slowly and quietly drifting away. How could I trust them to look after my son...

They had asked us to call all the family up to Leeds. They started arriving fairly early in the day, I don't think anyone had had much sleep.

Matthew was unconscious all that day, they wanted to wake him up to see if he had any brain damage. I knew he didn't because I'd seen him shake his head to me when we first arrived. I didn't want Matthew to wake up though, I didn't want him to know what had happened.

I was saying, 'Please don't wake him up' and they agreed to wait until later.

I recall thinking that I didn't want him to wake up ever. I wanted to protect him from knowing what had happened. Matthew was so active and doing so much and I thought, 'How could he go from that to being paralysed?' I'd rather he got a chest infection and faded away.

It was Chris who said we need to get him to wake up, they turned off the sedatives and it wasn't even 10 minutes before they came and got us.

Chris was in there chatting with him, I went in and was thinking, 'I can't stay here, I can't deal with this,' I remember wanting to run away. There was a hand behind me, gently pushing me, and I knew I couldn't run; Matthew needed me.

Chris: Someone had said that hearing is one of the first things that restores, so it was just inane drivel that I was saying to him, I was probably talking about the rugby or motor racing.

Glenda: Matthew couldn't talk, he still had the tube in his mouth. All he could do was blink to the questions asked by the doctor. I couldn't even get near him to give him a hug.

Unbeknown to us he'd been awake all the time he'd been injured. Matthew knew what had happened and the consequences of it. He had had to deal with it alone; I should have been there for him.

That was the bit I didn't want him to know, the part I wanted to protect him from. He obviously had a good understanding of what had happened but he was fading in and out of consciousness, in and out of oblivion.

He couldn't move and he couldn't talk, so the only way he could communication was just with his eyes.

The room that they tried to put us in first of all was what they called the relatives room. There were two sofas and we spent a lot of time in there. We weren't really doing much because Matthew was unconscious or sleeping a lot of the time.

There were two ward orderlies who were worried about us, they seemed to make it their mission to get us to eat. One of them made us some toast and tea. We looked at it, but just couldn't force it down.

Ten minutes later, the other lady came in, took the toast away, muttering it hadn't been made very well and returned a couple of minutes later with fresh toast on a plate. Everyone was so kind.

We were there with him all day and when we went back to the hotel that night, I did get some sleep. The next morning I must have looked so different, people almost didn't recognise me. My mum said my face was all twisted because I was so upset with everything that had happened.

BEFORE Matthew woke up, his dad and I both agreed that it would be better if he died rather than live a life in a wheelchair with that extent of disability.

I went up to the consultant and said, 'We've talked about this and we think that he shouldn't wake up.' Many ethical discussions followed.

Chris and I were in agreement that Matthew couldn't cope with being disabled. We were just doing what we thought was best for him.

What a wrong decision that was. Who were we trying to protect: Matthew or ourselves?

We had support from the RFL every day. Someone came in and sat with us and talked, mainly to Chris I think. It was someone different every day and the people who came seemed very uncomfortable with the situation. I don't think they really knew what to do, I don't think they had any training. They were men who worked in rugby, not with grieving parents in an ITU department in a hospital.

Chris: I always refer to the time before the accident as his first life into which he crammed in so much. He had everything going for him.

Glenda: They had to operate on the Tuesday and they were also trying to get him to breathe independently. You could see that as the day was going on he was really struggling.

There was someone from the RFL sat with Chris and I was with Matthew. He was really distressed and they were trying to get an anaesthetist to put him to sleep and insert a tube in his throat to help him breathe. Only the anaesthetist was busy. I stayed with Matthew, but it was really awful and I was on my own. Eventually I couldn't take it anymore, I left Matthew and got as far down the corridor as I could before the sobs started. Loud sobs. By the time I got to the relatives' room I was hysterical. I remember the poor man from the RFL completely out of his depth aware of the grief engulfing us and unable to do anything to help.

Matthew went to theatre that afternoon to add metalwork to his vertebrae to stabilise them. We walked into town. I was going to be brave. We got as far as the first department store. There were male mannequins with underpants. I just burst into tears, I didn't make it past the first shop. Matthew was always so proud of his body, his muscles, his trendy clothes.

But I thought, 'Pull yourself together you've got to go and buy something to wear.' I went into a shoe shop and got a pair of comfy shoes. The assistant was saying, 'Are you alright love?' Tears poured down my face the whole time.

But we did eat though- that was the first time we had eaten since Matthew had been hurt.

When we were with him, we were just grasping for anything, any sign that he was getting better. They kept on trying to wean him off the ventilator.

There was one little boy in the unit who was really ill. The nurses were shattered, emotionally and physically. You could see it in their eyes, in the way they spoke. You could sense how awful it was for everybody.

Chris: I went outside and the father of the child who was very ill came outside to have a fag and I was talking to him.

We later found out that the child had died and were thinking we were lucky because we still had Matthew, not in the way we wanted, but we still had him.

Over a period of time you begin to appreciate that it's better to have the Matthew that you've got – it's not ideal, but it's better than nothing.

Glenda: The day after his operation, Matthew became really poorly. He had pneumonia. They were having to do lots of physio for him, lots of antibiotics. Then his tummy stopped working and kept on getting bigger. They were saying they might have to take him to theatre, open it up until it stops expanding, so his organs weren't damaged.

I remember thinking, 'How much more is there going to be?' When will this nightmare end?

Matthew couldn't talk the whole time, he was just blinking. He could move his lips but no sound was coming out so to understand him you were having to watch him so closely. He seemed to get a lot of comfort out of having his head scratched and I can remember sitting there for hours just scratching his head while I was talking to him.

Chris went back down to work for a few days and I was up there with Matthew. I went early in the morning, and stayed literally until I got to the point where I couldn't do any more, I was totally exhausted.

On the Wednesday, his coaches came up to see him. They took us out into Leeds for a meal, that was the first time we laughed.

Some of his friends came up as well, so we saw lots of different people.

I was really lonely on my own. I wouldn't go down and eat anything in the evening at the hotel, I'd have something brought up – I was just going between Matthew and the room all the time.

In the morning, I would go down for something to eat. I was chatting to one of the ladies who worked there and told her what had happened and how poorly he was.

She said, 'He'll be alright love' but I just replied, forlornly, 'No he won't'.

She always sat and talked with me in the morning after that. She was so kind. People were so kind.

The days just merged into each other. We had a conversation with Matthew, saying 'No you won't ever walk again. Yes, you will be in a wheelchair, but it will be the biggest and fastest we can get for you'.

He never showed any upset. You could tell that he was down sometimes because he'd look distant.

Chris: With hindsight I don't think I coped, Glenda was the stronger one of the two of us. I came back home and went back to work. For me the work took my mind off things because I believe if you can influence something you should do, but if you can't...

Glenda: Medically, I had to remember everything and make sure Chris understood everything.

We were then trying to get Matthew moved down nearer to home.

As soon as he had recovered from his operation they started the process. He was very ill and I don't think I realised how poorly he was.

A bed became available at Luton and Dunstable for him and we thought that should be alright because it's next to the M1, they will know how to look after him.

The hospital were trying to get the air ambulance to take him down but they couldn't because it wasn't an emergency so they ended up arranging for him to be flown down to Luton Airport in a small plane. It must have cost a fortune because they had an anaesthetist and a nurse with him as well.

Chris: I was airside before the plane had landed. I wanted someone to be there who he recognised but I didn't know he was going to be asleep. He got put in the ambulance but even I couldn't go in with him so I tried to follow it.

Glenda: I've always been of the opinion that what happened, happened. I don't particularly want to have anything to do with Halifax in any way, shape or form because it happened there. I know it was an accident and we both agreed early on that it was, and we wouldn't blame anyone.

The manager from London Broncos arranged to visit

and I remember saying, 'You can come but you can't wear any clothing with London Broncos on it.' All through the visit I was checking to make sure he didn't have any logos showing.

Chris: The one thing that is ingrained deeply into my soul is when he was in Luton that night we were told we couldn't stay with him - they had visiting times!

As told to David Lawrenson

10.

Nearer Home

MY surroundings have changed. There is light coming in behind my head over my right shoulder. It is grey.

Whilst my mind had escaped to a world of tranquillity brought on by the sedatives, my body had made the journey from Leeds General Infirmary to the Luton and Dunstable Hospital.

There were familiar sounds, ones that had become my soundtrack; alarms, machines buzzing, the monotonous bellows of my ventilator.

That grey room, its appearance and the lack of life and atmosphere in it, was a metaphor for what my life had become.

Every 15 minutes, a thermometer was placed in my ear, my blood pressure measured, and vital observations recorded by the intensive care nurse stationed at the foot of my bed.

Unbeknown to me, I had been placed in a side room upon admission to minimise the risk of transferring any infection or virus I had picked up during my time in Leeds.

My family were with me and they sought to bring some normality to my existence through items from home; clothes, music and 'Piggy', my quasi cow/pig teddy bear which I used to practise my rugby passing on in my bedroom.

They also brought the many cards and letters of support which had been written in the weeks since my accident, from other family members, schoolmates reminiscing and strangers nationwide simply offering their support and words of condolence about what happened.

Such support was invaluable.

I remember the London Marathon playing out on the TV in my room; an event established to bring mankind together and to show what is possible through heart and determination.

It had the opposite effect on me, I could draw no inspiration, only comparisons.

My days had no structure, no meaning. Irrespective of how I had slept during the night, I would be woken for breakfast at 9am and offered toast, my only option. I declined it, without fail, every day.

My morning routine would see me bed-bathed by two nurses dressed in aprons and gloves. There was a radio on the shelf behind my bed, tuned to the local radio station 96.9 FM, and every morning around that time they played the 'Time Tunnel', a selection of songs from a given year which the audience had to work out before the DJ gave the answer later.

It was the one thing I looked forward to. I would lay

there, naked and vulnerable, and yet my brain wasn't on this intrusion to my dignity, it was on the challenge of working out the clues.

To escape, my mind focused on the smallest things to get me through.

Set menus came round for food ordering but I had no appetite, I was still being supplemented by a liquid diet through my nasogastric tube, and declined all options.

Mum would bring in meals from home; pasta, salad, crab sticks and prawns as had been my staple lunchtime meal at school. Yet, I had no desire for it.

She would feed me a few mouthfuls but I simply didn't want, nor could eat any more. I recall her occasionally pleading with me to at least try.

I was still very much in a state of ignorance with regards to my health, about what the machines and monitors were for, how they worked, and what would happen if one failed.

Having the ability to breathe when I wanted taken from my control was hideous. I would have panic attacks, believing I wasn't getting enough air and was suffocating. The more I panicked, the shorter of breath I'd become and the vicious circle would continue until I would be reassured by a nurse.

The lack of structure and purpose to my days was giving me an awful lot of time to think, reflect, and feel sorry for myself. I was a victim in all this and could not see the fairness of it all.

I did know that there was no recovering from the situation, however. It had been made clear to me by doctors that I had broken my neck, severed my spinal cord, and that it was unlikely I would see an improvement.

04.04.04

I was becoming more aware of what I had lost and that this life was different: one where I was confined, attached to machines and wires and dependent upon someone else for every one of my needs.

All I could think was, 'Bloody hell, Matt, you have really fucked this up for yourself.'

THE worst times were when I woke in the middle of the night. It was dark and quiet, with only the sounds of the machines keeping everybody alive breaking the oppressive curtain of silence.

It was then that I was more aware of my body and the pain I was in; my neck was still incredibly sore because of the surgeries and my tracheostomy a very raw wound in my throat.

This pain was exacerbated by the total lack of sensation I had below my neck; it was just a dull numbness.

I would lay there, and with every ounce of determination within me, attempt to awaken my body and shake it into life. Slow, concerted efforts at moving my little finger turned into rages of anger at its refusal to co-operate.

I was like a duck swimming against the tide; unseen my body was thrashing for all it was worth but on the surface, I was still as could be. I wanted, more than anything, for there to be something which could be done to alleviate the hurt, the numbness, the utter desolation that I felt.

A few days after I was transferred to the Luton and Dunstable Hospital, I woke in the middle of the night with terrible pain in my neck and was not getting the air I needed.

I was suffocating; desperation set in, followed by blind panic as I realised I couldn't attract anybody's attention and I would die here, in this coffin of isolation.

I started making the clicking noise I had learned. One click… Nobody came. Two clicks… Nobody came. Three clicks. Four clicks. Five clicks…

No matter how many times I clicked, the nurse remained seated at the station.

The small desktop light illuminating her face gave me hope but quickly that turned to exasperation as she looked away and continued with whatever was occupying her. My clicks continued to go unheard.

Eventually, she looked up from the nursing station, but this time maintained her gaze, pushed her chair back, and began walking towards me.

But, rather than taking the time to try and find out what was making me so frightened by reading the words I was desperately trying to mouth with my lips, she walked past my head towards the monitors positioned on the wall behind.

Having stayed there only a few seconds, clearly satisfied with what she had seen, she walked to the base my bed and, turning towards me, professed, 'Patience is a virtue,' before walking away and again taking her seat.

I was soul-destroyed. Again, I was alone in my world of pain and suffocation but now my feeling of panic had been replaced by fear. Fear that I could do nothing to influence my outcome.

I hadn't, before this time, realised that I was also dependent upon people who may not necessarily care about the personal nightmare I was trapped in.

My sense of vulnerability, triggered by this episode, was taken to a new level. I could not even trust those around me.

Something within me changed. Up to this point, I had

been confident in those charged to sustain and attend to my health and therefore felt it was my decision whether to live or die.

Because of this one episode, I knew I had to take ownership of my life.

I was ready to fight.

11.

New Life

MY time in the Luton and Dunstable Hospital came to an abrupt end. Every day, enquiries were made to the Royal National Orthopaedic Hospital, Stanmore, and the National Spinal Injuries Centre, Stoke Mandeville, in an attempt to locate a vacant intensive care bed I could be transferred to.

On the morning of 22 April, my treating Consultant, accompanied by my mum, stood at the bottom of my bed. When they were together, it was normally to convey bad news and it was with trepidation, anxiety and fear, that I awaited a further blow to my already shattered being.

To my surprise, mum took the lead in the conversation, stroking my head, and broke the news that a bed had been found for me at Stoke Mandeville and I would be moved later that afternoon.

She assured me that this was the start of my journey towards getting better, and eventually coming home again, whilst the Consultant gave assurances that Stoke Mandeville was the pre-eminent facility, not just nationally, but worldwide, for the treatment of spinal cord injuries.

As irrational as it may seem given this development, my only response was to begin crying. This transfer to my final destination in the National Spinal Injuries Centre made this whole situation real.

Despite everything I had been through, subconsciously I had been in denial up to this point.

Moving to the NSIC made me confront the irrefutable fact that my life had changed forever.

Mum stayed with me for a few minutes after the Consultant left; no words, just the rhythmic scratching of my head, needed to calm me down.

Preparations continued around me: machines, monitors, paperwork. This is what my life was now defined by and again I closed my eyes to try and escape reality.

IT is now dark. Oppressively dark. I have moved, but this is a multitude of steps backwards from what I am used to. There are no windows in this room, my surroundings are incredibly bleak.

I did not want to wake up in this dark coffin.

Keeping my eyes shut held inevitability off but only for the shortest of respites. The sedation had run its course and as much as I wanted to remain in a state of quasi-unconsciousness, my body would not comply.

When my eyes opened, I was not met by the familiar faces and sounds of my family. Just the artificial light flowing from the ceiling and an unfamiliar face in a nursing uniform taking my vital observations.

How long I was in this room I cannot say. Again, more

than ever, I was simply existing. There was no hive of activity, just a television at the foot of my bed, yet I could not sit up sufficiently to see the screen. It was simply a noise.

My parents and family were the only source of comfort I could draw from; the sole stimulation I had any inclination to make an effort for, the only thing bringing me out of the hell-hole of despair I was in.

I remember my parents and Michael being at my bedside. He was busying himself with some form of amusement or other and wasn't too interested in my plight. Strangely enough, I took comfort from how he still saw me as just his older brother. I did not want to be the centre of attention.

On this occasion, my parents had brought in a copy of the local newspaper, the *Biggleswade Chronicle*. It had been reporting on my injury since it had happened but this issue contained an article covering the success of my rugby team, Biggleswade U17s, in a national competition in Worcester.

They had won the tournament and had dedicated the victory to me. I was touched, but yet had to face up to the fact that I would never again play the sport I had loved all my life.

I could not tell you how long I lay in Intensive Care in Stoke Mandeville before my transfer onto St Andrews Ward, the High Dependency Unit. The time had come for me to truly take my first step on the road to recovery and it was unimaginably profound for me. It was the first baby step towards rebuilding my life.

St Andrews Ward is a 32-bed specialist spinal unit which caters for the most serious and high-level injuries, but is also a springboard towards the vital rehabilitation each patient requires as they continue along their path towards some form of recovery.

04.04.04

It is staffed mainly by Philippino nurses who send much of the fruits of their labour back home to their relatives. I found them to be charming, amiable and a source of companionship in this time of great loneliness.

Having made the short internal transfer, my home was to be in the six-bedded bay, with mine overlooked by the nursing station opposite.

There was a large bay window and no other patients.

Very quickly, my space began to reflect the love and support I had received since my accident; cards, photographs, paintings. Small gestures of kindness were placed on my bedside, pinned to the wall and adorned any and every spare inch available.

Whilst I couldn't even turn my head to look at them, it was comforting to have them near me, and to know I was not in this alone.

The battle had now taken on some structure, and there was a path ahead of me with a hopeful, but questionable, destination.

I was told I would recover my strength, or as much as was realistically achievable, eventually be transferred from St Andrews Ward onto a spinal rehabilitation one, return home and live a long, happy life.

It was all so easy to talk about, yet the reality was vastly different. A month on, there had been no improvement; I had simply moved destinations.

My routine in St Andrews Ward became familiar. I would be awoken at 5.00 am. Lights turned on, my bed sheet removed and a nurse, who I barely knew, would then insert suppositories to assist with my bowel management.

I would then be left in this position, supported by pillows, whilst I vacated my faeces onto the bed, such was the violation of my dignity. An hour would pass and, the bowel routine completed, I would be left awake, staring into the darkness of the ward and contemplating the bleakness of my future.

Everything had changed, even down to the clothes I could wear. Anti-embolism stockings to prevent deep-vein thrombosis, thermal bottoms, and a fabric corset to support my spine and prevent it bending. A bag in which my urine was collected was strapped to my leg, exposed to the world as it protruded from my tracksuit bottoms. I was unrecognisable.

Television was my saviour. Mum and dad had arranged for a portable TV stand on wheels to be brought up to the ward, and so began my love affair with daytime TV.

More than anything, *Neighbours* was the cornerstone around which my day was planned. Thankfully, at that time, it was shown twice a day on BBC1, and so our love affair blossomed.

How I would be distraught if an appointment or test of some sort would interfere with my scheduling.

I did, however, truly look forward to my physiotherapy and occupational therapy sessions. A schedule for daily therapies was written on a calendar and stuck to the side of the television and what this one bit of paper represented saved me.

Jo, my physiotherapist, was a regular face, kind and caring and would talk to me about everyday stuff, ordinary things which showed that life was continuing.

She would passively stretch each of my four limbs; aside from the circulatory benefits and maintaining range of movement, it was just good to see my body moving again. Yes, I was not controlling it, and yes, it did emphasise the

04.04.04

very extreme nature of the changes in my world but, nevertheless, seeing my fingers close to my face as Jo moved my elbows was just nice.

My occupational therapist, Erin, brought added light to the existence I was enduring, although I never really quite got my head around what was meant to be achieved in these sessions.

It mainly revolved around the care of my hands; it was explained to me that after a spinal cord injury it is imperative that the range of movement in my joints was maintained.

And so Jo concentrated on the wider breadth of my anatomy, whilst Erin seemed more than preoccupied with my hands. She made me hand splints which I had to wear every night – and still do – to keep my hands in the ideal position and she would stretch and rotate each individual joint and knuckle.

Up to this time, not a word had escaped my lips, not once had I been able to express my feelings, emotions or thanks, nor cry out in pain, despair, or through simple exasperation.

Smiles, tears, winces; these had become the outward embodiment of my inner turmoil. It was explained to me that my lack of speech was a short term, temporary affliction. Apparently, the tracheostomy in my throat was fitted with a balloon which expanded in my windpipe to prevent air escaping from around the tracheostomy site.

To help overcome this intolerable barrier barring my communication, I resorted to emphasising the movement of my lips and attempting to mouth the words I wanted to convey. Whilst a slow, frustrating and tedious process, both for me, my family and those caring for me, it was all I was left with.

An itch on my face became excruciating; no longer could I just reach up to scratch. It would build in intensity, becoming more intrusive as the minutes passed. If I did attract a nurse who could decipher my request, trying to describe exactly where it was became equally difficult.

When with my family or friends, I would listen to the conversations passing over and around my hospital bed.

I wanted to be involved but, more often than not, it felt as if I was being a hindrance. My attempts to say something would invariably bring the conversation to an abrupt end, as every face stared at me in silence and attempted to decipher what I was trying to say.

Not only had I lost the physical traits that made me Matthew King but I was quickly slipping into a world where it was easier to stay quiet; I was on a slippery slope to losing everything that made me, me.

After three weeks on St Andrews Ward, my world soon became one where noise was once again a possibility.

I had been coping well with eating and drinking and the oxygen saturation levels in my blood had remained consistently at a high level. That allowed more consideration to be given to deflating the cuff on my tracheostomy and thereby allowing air to pass over my vocal chords.

This was a monumental step and the significance of it was not lost on me. I appreciated that for the first time since my accident, I would be able to convey my emotions and desires, and begin engaging and interacting in the world around me.

I would no longer be a prisoner, trapped in this body and could vent the feelings that were building up inside me like a volcano, just waiting to explode.

It was on a doctor's morning round that the

consultants gathered around my bed, discussing the ramifications of trialing a deflated cuff.

I was incredibly scared of the consequences of the procedure failing but at the same time overcome with impatience to try.

That evening, the curtains were drawn and a female nurse approached me with a small 20ml syringe which she attached to a small clear pipe connected to the balloon in my throat.

'Stay calm Matthew, we can stop at any time, so blink your eyes twice if you need me too,' she said. And with that, she connected and pulled back on the syringe, removed the air from the cuff, and for the first time in six weeks, gave me the ability to speak once again.

'How does that feel Matthew? Are you in pain? Say something…' she implored.

'G…goo…Good. It feels good…,' was all I could muster but the relief in my eyes, and the smile on my face, was the only evidence they needed. It was a massive moment.

Mum's arrival in the evening started with her usual casual greeting of saying hello, and giving me a kiss on the forehead.

I replied, 'Hello mum… I'm good.'

She instantly responded, 'Good, how has your day been, Sunshine?' before the dots connected and she realised I had just spoken to her for the first time since 3 April.

Immediately, kisses, hugs and tears flowed, together with the realisation that my life had survived the darkest moments, turned a corner and started the upward climb along the hugely difficult road to recovery.

The next elephant in the room, as I saw patients moving around the ward in their wheelchairs, was having to face up to awful reality; of my new life as a disabled young boy in a strange, daunting and scary new world.

Given the amount of time I had spent lying on my back, it was necessary to begin acclimatising my body to sitting up again; I hadn't even contemplated that it would prove such an obstacle, but my first experience of doing so was truly awful.

Jo asked me if I was ready. Slowly the elevation of the hospital bed was increased, bringing my head away from the horizontal position to which I was now so accustomed.

Every degree the angle was inched brought with it further light-headedness as the blood ran from my head.

The peripheries of my vision were replaced by darkness and, as the seconds passed, it took a greater hold, removing all colour and clarity from my world, leaving only shadowy vague shapes.

My hearing failed me and was replaced by a dull ringing in my head.

I was unable to stop it. Consciousness drained away although I was aware of the frantic voices and movements of those around the bed.

All I wanted was for my body to be returned to the state with which I was now familiar.

Thankfully, as my head was once again lowered to the horizontal, my blood began its journey from my feet and my senses returned.

Whilst my mind wanted to take the first literal and metaphorical steps, my body was not yet ready to do so and my psyche took another jolt.

Jo asked me to try again the next day and assured me things would be taken slower. I was scared but said yes – I hadn't yet given up.

04.04.04

This time I was okay; whilst I could feel the effects of gravity, it wasn't as oppressive. At what equated to the level of sitting up in bed with a coffee and reading a newspaper, Jo stopped the incremental increases and told me that was enough for the day.

To my surprise, it was me pleading to carry on, to push my body to the limit of what it was capable but as the adrenaline began to wear off, I became more aware of the horrible sensations beginning to creep in and, after a short period, asked to be returned flat.

The sessions which followed brought with them improvements in not only my ability to tolerate this new vista with my head raised up, but also great strides in my frame of mind.

I had always been competitive, wanted to be a winner and as I overcame each progressive increase in the gradient of the bed, I could once again be proud of myself. I could now sit up in bed to face the world around me; to be able to look my family and friends in the eye was a huge wall I had climbed.

I was ready to take the next challenge; sitting in a wheelchair, even though the prospect of it was truly gut-wrenching.

I was told that the first time would magnify what I experienced when first sitting up tenfold. Not only would I need to summon all my will power not to submit to the light-headedness and nausea, but I would also need to take medication to help my body maintain its blood pressure.

A large green sling was placed under my back and between my legs which was connected to an overhead hoist to lift me from the bed and transfer me to the wheelchair.

My ventilator was unplugged from the wall, my head

supported with hands on either side and the wheelchair brought into position alongside the bed. It looked very crude and agricultural, with exposed metal pipes, worn out fabric covering the cushion and large rubber wheels.

I was told that I would propel it using a chin control which I would move forward, backwards, left and right with my mouth. To me, the wheelchair was a stranger, an unwelcome but necessary addition to my life.

AFTER weeks of immobility, this was to be the first time my body existed outside of a hospital bed. I was filled with trepidation, nervousness, excitement and apprehension.

One physiotherapist held my hands to stop them becoming entangled in the sling or my clothes during the transfer, whilst another applied pressure to the joystick controlling the hoist and slowly engaged its motor.

As my body was raised away from the bed, my neck muscles were unable to control the weight of my head, and but for the support of the physio, it would have hung loosely from the top of my shoulders.

My parents' faces were filled with love and willing support but I can only imagine their emotions as they saw their son being lifted and transferred into a wheelchair for the first time.

The hoist continued to raise me until my body was clear from the mattress. I was suspended in mid-air, the ceiling rails above my head engaged and I glided smoothly until I was positioned above the wheelchair.

I was slowly lowered into it and as my bum touched the cushion, the bones in the base of my spine began to take the pressure of my body weight.

I was sitting bolt upright in the wheelchair, with the

concerned faces of the family and physiotherapists looking on. But I felt fine.

My feet were positioned onto the foot plates, my arms and hands onto its armrests and the seatbelt applied. I was dipping my toes into the water of life in a wheelchair and physically and mentally, I was winning.

During the stifling heat of the summer, my days were spent slowly acclimatising to this new life, although my daily battle with hypotension was a long and draining one. Each time I was transferred into the wheelchair I vowed to survive a little longer before having to return to bed – and I did.

It was a dreary Wednesday morning when something which I had prayed for, but had ultimately lost hope of, became a possibility.

Having completed my morning routine and transferred into the wheelchair, the fingers on my left hand contracted into a balled fist of their own volition, with no input from anyone, relying solely upon my muscles and ligaments to do what I thought impossible.

Bewilderment and excitement overwhelmed me as I stared down at the armrest of the wheelchair. This was something the doctors had told me was an impossibility but in that moment, my life turned on a tangent – I had hope.

Every cautious, pessimistic piece of advice I had received to date was wrong, clearly. As loud as I was able to shout, I called for one of the nurses to come over and hopefully witness a repeat.

I waited, attempting to consciously control the movement of my hand. I stared down at my fingers, and with all my strength of mind, willed them to straighten themselves.

But my left hand remained non-compliant and curled

up in a ball. No nurse had yet come over and as the seconds passed, the near-euphoria began to subside, to be replaced by a huge dose of disappointment tinged with confusion, frustration and anger.

After months of tears, sorrow and resignation, that one movement had raised my expectations and possibilities, only to have them dashed in an instant.

As I was being put back in bed that night, I mentioned it to my nurse, Gordon.

'Don't be stupid, that was probably just a muscle spasm. It happens, so you should get used to it,' he said, matter-of-factly.

And with that, he blew my world apart; all hope that my body was repairing itself was dashed.

Having ventured as far as the ward balcony, the fresh air on my face welcome, in July - over three months after my injury - a visit to the spinal gymnasium came rather out of the blue.

Until then, my reliance upon the ventilator had delayed this quantum leap in my rehabilitation.

Unlike when merely exercising my limbs on the bed, Jo had access to much more equipment to make our sessions together more productive.

Whilst we would spend a good half an hour together concentrating on passive stretches of my limbs to ensure my muscles and ligaments didn't contract into unnatural positions, I was able to begin exercises that pushed my post-injury psyche and motivation to its limit.

Transferring into my wheelchair remained a daily difficulty but that had nothing on the effects brought on by the tilt table. No sooner were the motors that enabled it to become vertical engaged, than with every degree closer to

04.04.04

standing upright I became, the blood drained with greater velocity towards my feet.

Of much more long-term benefit were my neck strengthening exercises. The series of traumas and operations afflicting my neck had left me completely unable to turn my head of my own volition.

It was, effectively, a precariously positioned lead weight over whose movements I had little or no control. When in the wheelchair, my head would rest on its headrest and remain there until repositioned for me.

My long-term chance to control the wheelchair through my head movement was entirely dependent upon my ability to rebuild these muscles.

There aren't, however, too many conventional exercises or pieces of equipment designed to have this effect and so I was more than surprised when, on just my second visit to the gym, I was transferred from the wheelchair onto a padded flat table, and had straps attached around the entirety of my scalp.

To them was attached a long cable mounted on a system of pulleys, on the end of which were a number of lead weights that I would raise and lower through the movement of my head.

In effect, I was weightlifting, just in a slightly unconventional manner!

With every passing week, further weights were added until such time as I could hold my head upright and turn it independently.

Despite the discomfort of many of the exercises I attempted – and eventually overcame – in the gym, I treasured my hour per day in that room of torture.

It provided me with an escape and each success

brought with it a sense of pride and, in hindsight, a defining indication of my acceptance of my new life.

This stabilisation in physical condition rendered my stay on St Andrews Ward no longer a necessity, but rather a holding post until a ventilator bed became available on one of the three rehabilitation wards.

They are in such scarcity since they need to be in the line of sight of the nurse's station, and it was over a month of treading water before one became available.

The stark difference between St Andrews Ward and St Georges struck me on my first day in my new home. St Georges is an open, airy environment with doors opening onto an internal courtyard and is designed to be a bridge to eventual discharge back into the community.

More than anything, though, there was just more life. More patients moving about, more freedom and more wheelchairs. So many wheelchairs.

I still hadn't quite come to terms with what life in a wheelchair would mean and my time in one on St Andrews had been rather stationary.

St Georges was different; patients weren't confined to their hospital beds and dependent upon scheduled therapy sessions for their stimulus.

Here, they were less patients but people, and could now spend their free time either alone, with their family and friends, in the cafeteria, hospital gardens or close vicinity.

One of the first major developments in my long-term rehabilitation was my discharge planning meeting which took place in August, just a few weeks after my transfer downstairs to St Georges.

For most, this is a meeting attended by close family, a number of key individuals such as therapists and those from social services or the health authority responsible for the area to which the patient is to be discharged. Five or six people, maximum.

For me, that was not the case; being pushed along the corridor towards the meeting room, I could hear the chatter of conversation of those waiting for me.

As the door opened, there were 25 faces fixated on me, each I'm sure making a split-second assessment of the severity of my physical condition and gauging how this may impact upon their particular involvement in my path towards going home.

Being 17, there was a power struggle between children's and adult services, since, I'm sure, neither wanted to be responsible for the substantial financial responsibility for my on-going care, hence the numerous representatives.

Mum had used her nursing experience and determination to ensure that all those in positions of responsibility in the Bedfordshire Primary Care Trust, were there.

The discussion was centred primarily on my physical condition and how that would impact upon the level of care I would require to not only get home from hospital, but also in the days, weeks, months and years ahead.

In effect, they were all fumbling around blindly trying to make sense of the situation with little or no input from me.

Aside from being completely shell-shocked by the level of help I'd need to simply live from day to day, almost nothing was said which enabled me to constructively consider what it might mean, apart from one thing, my date of discharge; 10 November 2004. I would be out of hospital in four months, if all went to plan.

The date took on symbolic significance for me. It was

Full of beans:
My childhood
was a lively one.
Whether riding
my bike, paddling
in the sea, playing
football, starring
in a school panto
or hanging out
with my brothers,
I always seemed
to be full of mud
– or blood!

Oval ball game:
Once I began
playing rugby at
Biggleswade, *top*,
it became my life.

Growth spurt:
But I still suffered
from nightmares
and needed
comforting by my
younger brother,
not my proudest
moment! Having
put on a few
pounds, *above*, I
shed them again
in later years.

Making a splash: Enjoying Belgium's fountains on a school trip, exactly one week before my accident.

Getting serious: A tour down under with Bedfordshire Tigers in 2003 and joining London Broncos' Academy hinted at a bright future in the game.

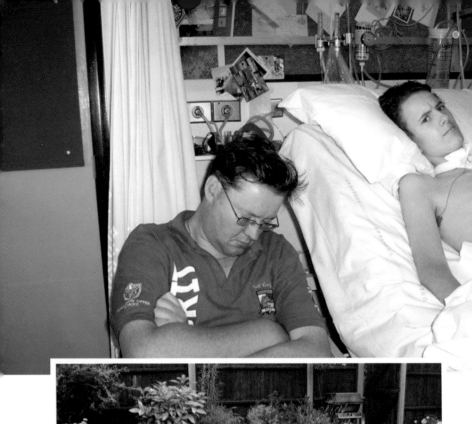

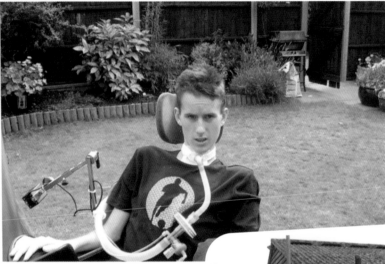

New reality: I may look grumpy as I lay in my hospital bed, but the days, weeks and months after the accident were hell on earth. Poor old dad looks shattered. My weight dropped hugely by the time I came home.

Right: Nugget was such a comfort to me in very dark times. Life can be so cruel.

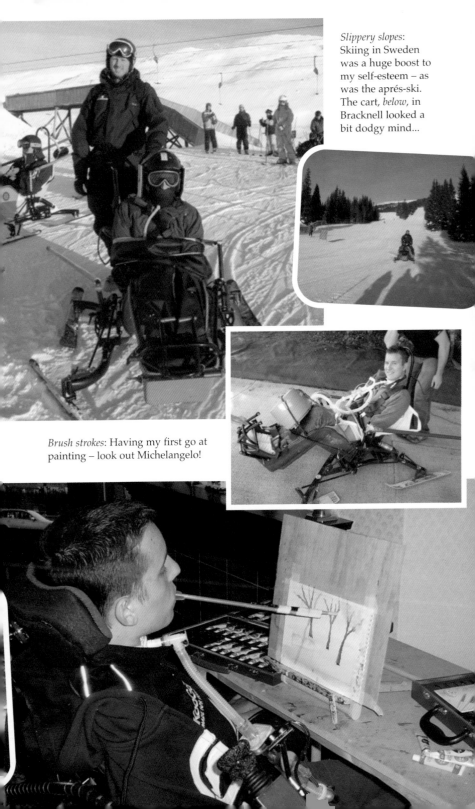

Slippery slopes: Skiing in Sweden was a huge boost to my self-esteem – as was the aprés-ski. The cart, *below*, in Bracknell looked a bit dodgy mind...

Brush strokes: Having my first go at painting – look out Michelangelo!

Sacred turf: What a treat it was to give a motivational talk to England's rugby league side before their encounter with Australia at Wembley in 2011...

Rugby league legends: ...and seven years earlier Australia's Kangaroos popped over to say hello during my first trip out of hospital.

Can we talk? Public speaking is now a big part of my life. Spoiler alert: don't look at the screen!

Don't stop me now: Taking part in – and finishing – the New York Marathon owed a lot to the brilliant support I received.

Cap and gown: I thought that I'd blown my law degree.

Going for gold: Here I am with the Olympic flame.

By Royal Appointment: I'm so glad that my family were with me at Buckingham Palace, where I was honoured with an OBE by HRH Prince Charles. The picture, *above*, is a little blurred – perhaps the photographer was shaking with the cold!

something to work for, a gateway into the new life I would lead.

It was now four months since my accident and my entire world up to this point had been confined to the perimeters of hospitals. I was yet to dip my toe in the waters of life as a disabled person, in the outside world.

Stoke Mandeville was a safe environment, one in which everybody had suffered a spinal-cord injury and we were taking the same journey. Outside, I would now be the exception, an anomaly.

Being seen as different, looked down upon, conspicuous, pitied even, terrified me; hospital had become a safe haven. But I went along with plans to go to a nearby pub, the Woolpack, as I knew it was something I had to do.

On a sunny Thursday lunchtime, for the first time, I was pushed through the exit doors of the spinal unit. Even to the other patients, I was different.

I had a long plastic pipe coming out of my neck connected to a large grey ventilator strapped to the back of the bulkiest wheelchair.

With dad pushing me and mum beside me, Jo carried a large backpack containing a seemingly endless list of emergency equipment and supplies, it was some expedition.

Waiting for me in the car park was a white Ford Transit van which had been converted into the spinal unit taxi.

Stopping the wheelchair just short of the tail lift, dad could sense my unease, I was so scared.

Slowly he pushed me forward onto the lift. I felt so incredibly vulnerable; for months I had been surrounded by hospital paraphernalia and support staff but now I was being raised into the air, with nobody to my left or right, no one holding my hand.

04.04.04

As we made our way through the village of Stoke Mandeville towards our destination, the jolts of the road, the inertia pressing on my body as we turned corners and the changing scenery were all so alien.

Arriving at The Woolpack, we came to a rest in the parking bay designated for the disabled. That was hugely symbolic, it differentiated me, more than anything, from my previous life.

It was a beautiful day and so rather than go inside, we sat in the beer garden. There were only a few customers outside, which was a relief. I could attempt to enjoy my first beer, free from the feeling of being stared at.

To go with a pint of Fosters, I had steak and chunky chips. As all our dishes arrived, dad put his to one side and came and stood beside me.

Despite my protestations that he eat his, he was determined to feed me that first chip. This was not something we could even contemplate weeks earlier.

I was only able to stomach a few mouthfuls but sitting in the garden, talking to mum and dad about absolutely anything but hospital was a joyous relief, and the return to the spinal unit came all too soon.

It was only that evening, having settled back into the monotony of the routine in the unit, that the stark comparison between my life in hospital and that of the outside world dawned on me, and I was able to reflect upon the possibilities in my life going forward.

That next taste came the following Saturday lunchtime. Mum and dad had, by this time, been trained to care for me and so, with Michael by my side, we headed into Aylesbury.

In the months since my accident, my hair had become

somewhat of a tangled mess and we decided that our trip into town would be with the aim of getting it cut.

We had the usual issue of parking and finding somewhere where we could site the van with enough room behind it for the lift to lower me to the floor.

I was anxious at the prospect of being in the midst of so many people and so was fairly vociferous in my denunciation of the plan and wanted nothing more than to head back to the safety of hospital.

Even in the van, I felt conspicuous and aware of my altered self-image and how I would look to other people. The parking bay dad found was literally in the town centre and so the process of getting out could not have been more bruising to my already shattered self-confidence.

My only way out was to close my eyes and deny I was at the centre of this unfolding drama.

In hindsight, we couldn't have thrown ourselves more into the deep end had we tried. As dad pushed the wheelchair through town, I was struck by how different life looked from this level.

I felt utterly worthless in this world which had once been so familiar and comfortable to me.

Being wheeled through Friars Shopping Centre, I became more self-aware and intimidated by those staring.

Dad was pushing the wheelchair but he had no way of sparing me from being an obstacle to all those in front and ploughed on irrespective of my protests.

We have a common trait of confronting an obstacle rather than avoiding it and it seemed to me that dad saw it as a point of principle to prove to others that we were just as entitled to move where we wanted, despite my mounting frustration.

04.04.04

Whenever we'd stop, I'd growl at him, pleading for him not to deliberately push the wheelchair at people but, of course, he told me he wasn't.

He was also new to all this and just as out of his depth. Having failed to find the hairdressers, we passed JD Sports, my favourite clothes shop, where I used to spend my weekly earnings.

Up to that point, whenever I had sat in the wheelchair in the spinal unit, I had worn a pair of Adidas flip-flops which I had bought for myself before the trip to Australia.

I thought they were pretty cool but they weren't really robust enough to protect my feet when out and about in the wheelchair and did nothing to keep them warm, and so I was told to invest in some decent footwear.

Entering the shop, I immediately saw that the clothes rails were quite close to one another, making the space for the wheelchair to pass too narrow and doing nothing to allay my frustrations.

There was no way of getting through the shop without having somebody go in front of me and move the clothes from my path, like macheteing through a jungle, and given I had absolutely no desire to make such a public exhibition of myself, I wanted no part of it.

Surprisingly, while contemplating our entry, Michael had moved one of the clothes stands far enough from the front of the shop for dad to back the wheelchair into the corner of the store.

That not only gave me enough space to try on the new shoes, but also a degree of privacy. We were all beginning to come to terms with these new challenges.

12.
Inspiring Gesture

LIFE in St Georges Ward continued in this vein. Daily therapy sessions intertwined with pre-planned excursions from the hospital. Everything I did was focused on 10 November, I could not wait to get home – or so I thought.

Deep down, in the recesses of my being, I was also terrified of leaving hospital. I was in danger of becoming institutionalised.

My time in St Georges also brought with it a peculiar tendency for my clothes to go missing, which did not amuse me.

They were part of my identity and linked me to my previous life. Waking up in the morning, I could never be certain that my clothes wouldn't pass before my eyes on the body of another person.

Ted, a fairly elderly gentleman with Down's Syndrome and the kindest of hearts, had slipped in the

04.04.04

shower a few weeks earlier, broken his neck and ended up in the bed opposite me.

He was a short man, with a sparse head of ginger hair and a truly inquisitive nature. On one occasion when mum was readying herself to take me from the ward to the cafeteria, Ted saw her preparing my suction machine and emergency equipment and, in the softest, and most uninhibited of tones simply asked if he could come.

She did not hesitate to agree as she knew what a difference a few minutes away from the usual environment could make to a man who had few visitors and very few highlights in his day.

Whilst a fragile man, Ted did have the determined strength to push his own wheelchair and so the three of us, with Ted leading, headed from the ward.

Mum had a coffee, Ted and I hot chocolates and we all had toasted teacakes. That meant mum had a predicament: three mouths to feed, but only one pair of hands.

She helped prepare and feed Ted first, his eyes with a real glint in them as he sat surrounded by other families, amongst the hubbub and atmosphere so devoid on the ward.

One morning, I asked the health care assistant to dress me in the same clothes as I had worn the previous day; my black Adidas tracksuit bottoms and Saracens rugby shirt which had been given to me by the club's owner Nigel Wray when he had visited me out of the blue.

I had worn it almost every day since and was more than surprised to hear that my chosen attire wasn't on the trolley next to my bed where they had been put the evening before. The nearby cupboards were searched high and low, but my garments were nowhere to be seen.

Resigned to defeat and having asked the staff to ring

134

mum to bring in fresh clothes, when Ted's curtain was pulled back, there he was, laying on the bed, swamped in my gear.

I didn't see the funny side, whatsoever. As time drew on, so my anger subsided to more of a simmering annoyance and given the beaming smile spread across Ted's face, I didn't have it within me to demand the return of my clothes.

Of a far more sinister nature, my clothes were again to disappear just weeks later. This time, it wasn't an innocent misunderstanding, it was theft.

Olga, the ward's resident recluse, was also, as I found out to my detriment, a lady with few morals and no conscience.

She had a fairly chequered past. A Bulgarian national by birth, it appeared that Britain's immigration policy meant little to her and having made her way here, she was determined not to leave.

A 30-foot drop from a bridge over the M25 was a hurdle in her path to escape the authorities and it left her with a broken back, custody at her Majesty's pleasure, and a stint in the National Spinal Injuries Centre.

She quickly developed a reputation as a bit of a loose cannon. She spoke no English, was a fairly intimidating lady and was allocated a side room on the ward, which she decorated with the plastic flower display stolen from the unit's foyer.

And rather than being used as the soft lining for orthopaedic corsets which patients used to support their trunk, the store of sheepskin inserts in the spinal gym were quickly identified by Olga as ideal carpeting for her floor.

One night, Olga was slowly walking down the corridor past my hospital bay; whilst she had broken her back, she had only partially severed her spinal cord and so was able to get by with the aid of crutches.

04.04.04

She was dressed in another of my favourite rugby shirts, mocking me as she passed in the knowledge that I could do nothing about her stealing my identity.

A frantic search ensued when, in autumn 2004, she went missing. Searches of her usual haunts proved fruitless and there was a real concern that a lady with a broken back had managed to circumvent Britain's watertight immigration laws.

Having done a rudimentary search of my hospital bay, Victor, a pleasant nurse from Africa, opened the curtains of the door leading onto the internal courtyard.

He then let out a bloodcurdling scream. In the pitch darkness, he had been set upon by one of the ghosts rumoured to walk the corridors of the hospital or rather Olga, covered in a white bedsheet, waiting to ransack the first unfortunate individual to come across her.

LIFE in Stoke Mandeville Hospital was manageable during the day.

Distractions brought the smallest respite from the automatic reflections upon my life and how my prospects had changed so completely in the previous six months. Such thoughts would invariably dominate my outlook and as much as I knew this would not change my situation, it was an inescapable virus damaging my psyche.

Mum and dad's resolve to ensure I didn't give up the fight to convalesce, or let me wallow in my circumstances, was a constant presence; some would call it tough love, but it was exactly what I needed.

They sympathised and empathised but not for one second did they treat me any differently.

Whilst I saw myself as the victim in all this, they were

determined that we, as a family, would make the best of the situation.

Mum had by now taken a sabbatical from work to give her time to fit in all of the competing elements of her life. Michael was 12 years old and much like most children of that age, needed a good deal of direction to keep him on the straight and narrow.

He went slightly off the rails, with less than glittering school reports, unscheduled partying and a general lack of interest in most things.

Mum would update me about goings on at home and in the village and, craving stimulus, I would pine for life in the outside world.

My bed in hospital was in a predominantly male area of the ward, the other patients a great deal older than me.

Despite our predicaments, there was still the usual bravado which was another reason I needed mum's presence.

Having her there allowed me to get away with watching – and thoroughly enjoying – *Grease* and *My Big Fat Gypsy Wedding* while using her as the necessary excuse for having to 'endure' them.

Aside from the weekend, dad's visits were confined to evenings after work.

They were usually accompanied by fish and chips from the local chippy down the road and brought back pleasant memories of travelling back from Bedfordshire County rugby practice on a Wednesday evening and stopping at a chip shop in Flitwick on the way home.

By the time dad arrived in the evening I would have long before gone back to bed, and we would talk about pretty much anything but our current surroundings.

In the absence of mum and dad, there was a strict rota

system put in place between grandparents and family on both sides, which ensured that in the totality of my hospital stay, I spent only two days without seeing a familiar face.

STRANGERS held a position for me in their hearts. Waking up in the morning, I would always look forward to the post and receiving their letters which brought light into my days.

Craig, a producer of toiletries in Halifax, sent me numerous parcels without ever having met me; he symbolised such kindness.

The teachers from Stratton Upper took it upon themselves to take it in turns twice a week to bring a car load of students in to see me after school. It was a good three hour round-trip, and I knew, in my heart, that I could not and would not give up on myself if others hadn't.

I was so incredibly fortunate and it meant such great deal to know I wasn't in this alone.

Growing up, there was always an open biscuit tin in grandma's house and now that I was in hospital, nothing had changed. She and her second husband Tony took it upon themselves to not only keep me well stocked, but also feed most of the ward.

Once I had had my fill of whatever delights they had brought in, usually from my favourite 'The Hot Shop' they'd walk around the ward offering them to anyone who fancied a treat.

Gran and grandad had owned a sweet shop in Hitchin during my formative years and my Saturday highlight was helping behind the till for half an hour or so. As a reward, I earned a 50p bag of sweets and never lost the taste for them. My hospital bed was always filled with all my old favourites.

Andrew's visits were always a source of great delight. It was nice to see him, but what was of more interest was the seemingly constant turnover of females he brought with him.

Never one to miss an opportunity, the fact that he could demonstrate his caring side by bringing his conquests into hospital to visit me must have been a feather in his cap.

The nights remained long, dark, lonely hours surrounded by machines, strangers and the oppressive reflections upon my life.

Waking up, I found it impossible not to think about my past, present and, more painfully, my future. More and more the wheelchair, the ventilator and my paralysis were encroaching in on my dreams.

My one saviour in those night time hours was Tracey Geddis. Nurse Tracey is one of those people who simply care.

I would spend many an hour listening, talking with or battling to save my Haribos from her.

Once all of the evening rounds had been completed, the lights turned off and the patients settled for the night, as I would lay awake, Tracey would pull up a chair and sit next to my bed.

She would tell me about ex-patients she had cared for who had gone on successfully to rebuild their lives, or light up my evenings with tales of her experiences with the Backup Trust, a charity established to help people living with a spinal-cord injury fulfil their potential.

But, more importantly to me at that time, were her tales of the outdoor activities organised by the charity.

Tracey's partner is in a wheelchair and had previously been on skiing holidays to Sweden with them.

Although just a dream, I allowed myself to indulge in the possibility that one day it might be possible for me too.

Kayaking, abseiling, sailing – it began to dawn on me that there were opportunities far beyond sitting in a wheelchair all day for the rest of my life.

Those times spent listening to her began to plant the seeds of hope in the back of my mind that it would be possible to enjoy my life again.

The foundations on my long road to recovery were laid in those early hours of the morning, which I began to build on with every session in the gym, every hour with my therapists and every tentative excursion into the outside world.

In the absence of having anybody else in the unit with my level of injury to speak to, I did have one person I could look towards and strive to emulate. Christopher Reeve, the *Superman* actor.

Like almost every child my age, I had grown up with those films and whilst before my accident I had only been vaguely aware of Reeve's disability, my newfound situation brought his predicament into sharp focus.

Reeve had broken his neck in 1995 following a horse riding accident and was left in an identical physical state as myself, paralysed from the neck down and dependent upon a ventilator to breathe.

Despite that, he continued with his life, directing films and pioneering what was possible.

He had become my target, my focus. He gave me hope, inspiration, and more than anything, I was intrigued to see if I could emulate his success. That is until 10 October 2004.

Reeve's death was breaking news on the television, radio and on the lips of everybody in the unit when I awoke. While it was obviously an enormous tragedy for those who knew and loved him, it was also yet another kick in the teeth for me. Laying there in bed being washed and dressed during my morning routine, I was once again alone. 'If Superman cannot beat this, how can I?' was all I could think.

But my progress continued.

Waiting in bed for my physiotherapy session to begin, Jo came in pushing the usual wheelchair but there was something different about it.

A series of horizontal bars had been fitted to the back, to which was attached what looked like a computer console joystick. It was explained that this would be the only way in which it would be possible for me to drive it independently. This was a huge development.

Once my body was aligned into position in the chair, Jo undid the screws securing the joystick in place and manoeuvred the bars until it was immediately in front of my chin.

Amid the mix of excitement and trepidation, it was explained to me that the driving system was relatively simple; I would push up on the joystick to go forward, hold down to go backwards and manoeuvre it to the left or right to change the wheelchair's direction accordingly.

Tentatively, I pushed up slightly with my chin and the chair crept into action. Centimetre by centimetre, metre by metre, I moved forward down the corridor with a harem of clinicians, nurses and healthcare assistants walking behind me.

I was like a boy playing with a new toy, and I wanted more speed. Of course, my pleadings were met with the sensible response that I should take it carefully.

I drove the wheelchair the short distance to the gym and was met with words of encouragement, support – and warnings about my driving – as I passed the now familiar faces in the spinal unit.

Strangely, a feeling of pride began to surface within me, an emotion I had not experienced in such a long time.

My newfound freedom did not extend to exploring any areas within the ward not in eyesight of the nurses station and so my practices consisted primarily of straight-line drag races in front of it.

I could, however, extend these boundaries when with mum as, by this time, she had completed her in-house training as to how to care for me.

At every opportunity, I would jump at the chance to move away from the side of my hospital bed.

Exploring the confines of the ward on an ordinary day in October 2004, I sensed that my body had become very cold – an unusual sensation now as my nerve endings had been disconnected from my brain.

Fortunately, grandma had bought me a wheat pad that could be heated in the microwave for just such an eventuality.

Having asked mum to warm it and place it behind my neck, as she did so, my face was pushed forward onto the chin control and, unable to move my head away, the joystick was forced forward and the wheelchair took off.

Mum and the nurses screamed and there were looks of horror on the faces of those I quite majestically passed.

Catching me first, mum instinctively grabbed the handles on the back of the wheelchair but was soon a passenger as the torque of the motors dragged us along.

Attempting to extricate my face, the joystick followed and the wheelchair veered to the left, careering into the wall with my exposed feet acting as the impromptu crumple zone.

This did nothing, however, to break the connection between my face and controller and the wheelchair continued to gouge a deep rift in the decorations whilst heading towards the exit.

But my path was blocked by the not so insubstantial presence of a patient sitting in his wheelchair. The inevitable collision came, and with our feet mangled and intertwined, I came to a shuddering halt.

Extracting himself slowly, the disgruntled victim turned his wheelchair, declined all offers of help and wheeled himself away from this scene of disarray, leaving me half-embedded in the wall.

As 10 November drew closer, it became more apparent with each passing day that I wouldn't make my goal of being discharged that soon.

There were adaptations to be made to our family home in Langford, medical equipment and wheelchairs to be bought and a care regime to put in place.

There was, however, something else on the horizon I could look forward to.

The 2004 Rugby League Tri-Nations tournament between England, Australia and New Zealand was being played over here and I was invited to the match between Australia and New Zealand at QPR's Loftus Road.

Although, if Aylesbury town centre on a Saturday lunch-time had been difficult, then negotiating 20,000 rugby fans did not fill me with excitement.

To keep out the cold, I was dressed in layer upon layer of thermals and jumpers, whilst coats were applied until I was simply too big to fit in a wheelchair. There were hasty, but necessary adjustments made before I could sit relatively comfortably in it.

04.04.04

The journey to Loftus Road was by far the longest I had endured and sitting in the wheelchair in the adapted Ford Transit as we made our way to the stadium, I felt sick to the stomach. I was scared of how I looked to other people, how they would react to me.

I wanted to turn around and was grateful for every traffic jam that delayed our arrival.

We got there an hour before kick-off amidst the throng of spectators making their way into the ground.

There was no side street on which to park from where I could discreetly leave the vehicle, rather, we alighted immediately outside the stadium and my exit on the wheelchair lift was seen by the hundreds of fans passing at that moment. To me, it was gut-wrenchingly awful and embarrassing.

The heavens then opened as dad pushed me towards the wheelchair enclosure in the nearmost corner of the ground, and I arrived cold, wet, and thoroughly pissed off.

I was watching the teams warm up when an unfamiliar face came up to me and introduced himself as Chris Hawkins.

In the weeks leading up to the match, there had been more and more talk of a chap embarking on a fundraising bike ride from Leeds for me who was aiming to arrive at the stadium just in time for kick-off.

Chris had started off earlier the previous morning and endured rain, wind and sleet to make it and be alongside me as the match began.

Introductions hastily completed as the ball soared, it very quickly became apparent that Chris was a hard-core rugby league nut and loved everything about the game.

My speech at the time was still incredibly weak and

when combined with the noise within the stadium, it was hard to even hear myself when I spoke, let alone expect anybody else to.

Despite that, Chris chatted with me, not just about the game, but his cycle ride and my experiences playing and we clicked instantly. He did not tiptoe around me and avoid what I perceived to be an awkward subject, but instead I sensed very quickly that he simply saw me as Matt.

Chris had never met me before, never seen me outside of a wheelchair and without the ventilator, but he looked through all this. Banter and inappropriate jokes were hit back and forth like a tennis ball across the net and the match passed by in a flash.

Looking back, I guess I believed that everybody would now see me as I saw myself, completely changed from the person I had been and lacking in any confidence, charisma or character.

But in that one meeting with Chris, I knew my instincts had been wrong and I was relieved and elated that others could still see the remaining fragments of the person I am.

The match finished and Chris, his partner Lesley, my family and I remained in the wheelchair enclosure for a few minutes.

I just thought we were letting the crowds die down before we headed back to the van, but I was wrong.

The Australian team were making their way around the pitch waving to their supporters and thanking the crowds.

For me, it was a thrill to be so close to these players who, for most of my life, I had dreamt of emulating.

I felt rather inferior to all those around me screaming

for their attention but rather than walk past where I sat, the players, as a group, turned and began walking towards me.

Chris, standing next to me, was almost exploding with excitement and I sensed that I hadn't been told the whole story. The players climbed over the metal railings, knelt down and started speaking to me; Willie Mason, Anthony Minichiello, Shane Webcke... my idols were chatting to me like it was just an ordinary thing to do.

I was overwhelmed, and the huge smile which spread across my face was not something that had surfaced for a long, long time.

I was invited by the Kangaroos coach Wayne Bennett into their changing room. There was no easy way to do this; Loftus Road is an old stadium, not exactly cut out for large powered wheelchairs to manoeuvre around.

Whilst it continued to lash down with rain, dad pushed me around the perimeter of the pitch until we reached the players tunnel on the far side of the stadium.

Entering, I passed BBC pundit Ray French, who, surreally to me, knew who I was and was happy to chat about the match.

This was all getting rather incredible and on entering the Australian dressing room, Wayne Bennett and I chatted away as if this was the most normal experience in the world.

The over-powering smell of Deep Heat and sweat took me back to my days on the pitch with my teammates but, for the first time, I no longer pined after the life I used to lead. I was, at least, becoming acquainted with this new version.

After that, I was lifted down a set of stairs in the wheelchair by four of the New Zealand squad and sat in the van speaking with Lesley Vainikolo, the Kiwi winger, who had come out into the street to see me.

It was an incredible day and gave me the final impetus to get out of hospital and begin living life.

THE reality of what the future might look like hit home when interviewing potential candidates to form part of my day-to-day care team. I was analysing adults twice my age and assessing their suitability to fulfil a role that I had absolutely no comprehension of.

I had no way of gauging whether they would be good at their job and simply went on gut instinct of whether I believed I could get on with these people 24 hours a day, seven days a week.

In all, I undertook 15 interviews over a one-week period and accepted eight applicants.

Over the days and weeks which followed, I trained each support worker in every facet of my looking after.

Having to teach each of them how to perform my bowel care and drain my urine was a horrible, dignity-sapping experience. I was also having to learn to converse with adults of different nationalities, cultural backgrounds, and intellectual abilities and, as a 17-year-old boy, this was probably the most difficult element of the transition home.

Bizarrely, after only a week, I had to sack a rather elderly lady who, whilst assuring me she could hear perfectly well, was actually stone deaf; hardly conducive to hearing alarms going off or my clicking for attention.

And so it was that after 258 days, 6,192 hours, my hospital stay ended. On 17 December 2004, I was allowed home.

The night before was entirely sleepless. Every turn of events in my life played themselves out in my mind.

I was on the precipice, at the tipping point, which the

following day would see me enter a life I had never anticipated, wanted nor expected, but one which was in my hands to make the best of.

By the time my support workers arrived at 9am, I was fully dressed and had been in the wheelchair for an hour.

My blood pressure had time to stabilise and I even took the opportunity to indulge in a final breakfast; I rather enjoyed my first taste of Marmite in nine months.

This was truly a day of mixed emotions. I was excited and eagerly anticipating life in the outside world, but was equally daunted and terrified by the prospect of it.

I was looking forward to escaping this world of doctors, nurses, and therapists but, equally, would miss them. There would be no more physiotherapy or occupational therapy sessions, no more clinical assessments and I would miss them too.

They had become my life and were, on the whole, positive experiences where I once again had purpose, drive and ambition.

Being pushed by one of my new support workers to say my goodbyes was nerve-wracking.

I was scared to leave the safety of hospital and the relationships I had built. I was overcome by tears and fear when saying goodbye and thank you to my therapists. But there was no going back.

Equipment loaded and support workers in tow, I departed from St Georges Ward, into the foyer of the National Spinal Injuries Centre and out of its exit doors for the final time.

13.

The Return

AS I prepared for a new life at home, so did my parents and family. Without their support, perseverance and positivity, it would never have happened.

They recall getting from Leeds to that point.

Glenda: Once Matthew had arrived at the Luton and Dunstable hospital he was settled in a side room, in case he had picked up any infection from Leeds.

Our first interaction with the unit was someone preventing us from entering to see him, telling us to wait until they decided they were ready. I know they had a job to do but all I wanted was to let Matthew know we were there for him, for me to make sure he was OK. Rules are rules though.

We were only able to visit for short periods. The first morning there, I remember playing 'Build Me Up Buttercup' by The Foundations, one of his favourite songs, quite loudly.

04.04.04

Lots of Matthews's friends started coming to see him once he had been transferred to Luton. They were anxious moments for us, how will they react when they see him and he with them? Good friends are always there though.

I don't think we ever felt really safe with Matthew at Luton. I can remember us ringing the ward every morning to see how he was and he'd never had a good night's sleep. He was obviously quite agitated in there.

Every time you change to a different environment you lose all that confidence in the staff and you have to build that up again. You can only know that by testing them and seeing that they do know what they're doing.

The visiting times were really awkward; you could go between midday and 2pm and then 4pm and 6pm. Luton to Biggleswade took about an hour so there wasn't time to come back home in between.

We needed to be with him all the time, so we just used to hang around. It was really awkward and no one was aware that it was really difficult for us. Nobody really spoke to us.

I seem to remember thinking that Luton and Dunstable would be quite safe because it was by the M1 and they'd be used to and have an awareness of trauma and spinal injuries but I'm still not convinced that they did.

Matthew had a really horrible night once, one of the staff couldn't communicate properly with him and so didn't give him the care and support he needed. That was a really bad time and he didn't sleep for days after that.

As parents, you are in a very difficult position. If you complain, then Matthew is at the mercy of everybody there. Part of you thinks, 'Are we being over-protective?' Then you think, 'That's my son, how dare you be horrible to him?'

The impact of that one night on Matthew – and on

us – remains with me still. If I ever met the person involved, I don't know what I would say or do.

We didn't actually complain until he was transferred to Stoke Mandeville, which happened a few days later.

We wrote to the ward sister, saying we didn't think Matthew had been looked after very well that night. The response, he could be demanding...DEMANDING.

His life, as he knew it, had been blown apart. No longer able to move, speak, do anything. In an ITU unit, allocated at least one person to be with him all the time, and you think he was demanding? That's when I really got involved, how dare she?

The outcome of my complaint, additional training for staff. How can you train someone in basic human kindness?

When they finally had a bed at Stoke Mandeville, they blue-lighted him over there and the first time I ever broke down was that initial day at Stoke. We'd been fighting to keep him safe up to that point.

We met the consultants later that day and, having examined him, that was when they told us the likelihood of any improvement was virtually nil. That was obviously a really bad time.

On the way home the tears started, and flowed and flowed. When people say their heart is breaking, I know exactly what they mean. It hurt really badly, physical as well as emotional pain.

We were focused on getting him off the ventilator - if he could do that then at least he'd have some independence.

I remember one of the sisters on the ward having trouble dealing with it saying, 'He's so young and so handsome, he's got to be able to breathe'. She was really caring but it wasn't very helpful hearing her saying that.

04.04.04

Matthew wouldn't sleep. They were giving him injections probably every two hours to try to get him to go off . He was so terrified by that stage which I'm sure went back to Luton and Dunstable hospital.

I can remember him saying to us, 'You should have let me die'. That was the only time he's ever said it.

The spinal unit at Stoke Mandeville was quite gaudy, it had bright red carpet and a big display of artificial flowers in the middle. There were bright green stairs going up to the floors and dark brick work. I've had to go back a few times since with work and I just hate going in there – it wasn't what you'd expect to see.

A lot of the nurses had English as their second language and they used to communicate between themselves in their own language quite a lot, often going down the ward giggling, which was difficult.

Matthew's way of dealing with it, once he was able to speak again, was to get them to teach him their language. They used to give him individual words which he would repeat. We were never quite sure what they were telling him, as they would often walk off laughing afterwards!

In the first few days Matthew went down to theatre a few times. He had problems with his tracheostomy site that they were trying to sort out, there was always one problem after another. You just really went from day to day.

I would sometimes drive over to see him, only to learn he was going back down for further surgery. Nobody bothered to tell us.

I didn't really want to see him being put in his wheelchair for the first time but I did stay with him. It looked really horrible and was battered around the edges. That was a reality check, and quite a low moment. The thought of him

152

in that chair, that this was what the rest of his life was going to be like, it was horrible.

When they put him in the chair his blood pressure dropped, he looked absolutely dreadful and he passed out.

The first time we took him out it was so scary.

First of all we had to learn to use the ventilators and I remember saying to Chris, 'I can't do this on my own.' We both learned together all about the machines and how they worked. Even Michael wanted to be involved, to be able to do something for his brother.

There was a pub a couple of miles away that the staff suggested we took him to. We drove there in the hospital van, wheeled him in and then realised we needed to take his coat off.

We were trying ever so hard to do it right but you could tell that Matthew wasn't really sure that we knew what we were doing. I remember very clearly saying to him, 'We're doing our best.' We just didn't have the skills we needed to look after him.

Then we had to feed him his meal. Eating is such a social activity, but not then. We'd done it in the hospital but never in public before. It felt very odd and, in the background, we were terrified about this ventilator and whether it was going to carry on working and what we would need to do if not.

There was one day when I went in and Matthew decided he wanted to go and watch the games that were on at the stadium they had there attached to the hospital.

He wanted me to take him on my own but he needed to have two people looking after him all the time so I wouldn't do it.

Matthew was furious with me. He drove off in his

wheelchair and in his temper crashed into the nurse's station. His frustration at his situation was clear for us all to see.

Chris: We took him down to Queens Park Rangers' ground in London to see a rugby league Tri-Nations game with Australia. We were petrified driving down there but eventually found somewhere to park and watched the game.

We were in the bottom right hand corner of the ground and on the final whistle the Australian team, led by their coach Wayne Bennett, came across to see Matthew. They climbed over the barriers and the whole team surrounded him. Sky Sports were waiting to interview them but it was like, 'No we've got something more important to do' – they treated Matthew like one of their own.

Then later some of the lads climbed into the back of the van and all the fans outside were wondering what the hell was going on.

Lots of people came to see Matthew. There were car loads from school who would talk the inane drivel that teenagers do, but just having them there for him was huge.

Glenda: We all had the goal of Matthew coming home. Soon after he was admitted to Stoke Mandeville, they started the discharge planning process.

I had to go back to work and found it really tiring leading two lives. I explained to them I needed to wean myself off going to see Matthew every day – that was the hard bit because I'd been so protective of him.

We discussed Matthew coming home and I said to Chris, 'He'll just have to come into our dining room.' Chris thought I'd lost the plot. He went down to see the discharge team saying, 'Glenda's talking rubbish' – he thought I'd gone a bit loopy at that stage. But Matthew did come home at Christmas and he did come into our dining room.

Matthew had a home visit in June or July. The occupational therapist at Stoke was leaving and she decided she wanted Matthew to come home before she did. That was the target.

The RFL took a photograph of him that day. He looks absolutely dreadful because he'd lost so much weight and was probably down to about seven or eight stone. We could see him losing it in front of our eyes.

Chris being Chris, he decided he would be bringing his son home himself so he drove over to Stoke from work – which took an hour – brought him home and then had to repeat the process to take him back. All the family came to be with Matthew on his first trip home. All he wanted was sausage and chips!

We had to change our doors at the back of the house into the dining room because we had sliding patio ones and they wouldn't have been wide enough for Matthew to get through. One of our friends had a double glazing firm and he pushed the work through so we had it done in a couple of weeks to allow this first visit.

It was lovely.

We had huge support from the NHS who arranged the carers he needed on his return home. Without that we couldn't have got him back. He needed a big care package and they recruited trained people specifically to look after him.

Obviously it would be much cheaper to the NHS for Matthew to be looked after in a care home. That was a huge worry but we were totally committed to him coming back to us.

04.04.04

We went to see Alistair Burt, our local MP, and he was really helpful and supportive and did some background work to make sure it happened.

Matthew came home for weekend leave first of all, a couple of weeks before Christmas. We picked him up on the Friday and he went back on the Monday. There was a bit of to-ing and fro-ing as we hadn't actually got a discharge date.

We took everything out of the dining room which was to become his bedroom. We got the hospital bed and added shelves to the room for storage. We also had to clear Matthew's bedroom for the carers to sleep in. That was really hard. Chris was outside working one day and I just went in and did it. I cried all the way through.

The first weekend was really scary because we had carers in our home, two on every shift. They knew the theory but not really the practice. You had people in the house 24 hours a day; they were working and we were trying to live there.

It was quite bizarre, you had to get on with your own life and yet there were these people there all the time.

We couldn't have a row, you had to be on your best behaviour all the time.

Chris: His brothers Michael and Andrew were getting caught up in it and poor old Michael was the one who suffered. He really lost out because there was a major lack of emotional support available to him because Matthew was sucking it all out of us. Andrew was that little bit older and was much more independent.

Michael was very much on the coat tails and pulled along. It was what Matthew wanted that mattered and that was really hard for him. It took many years for poor old

Michael to understand what was going on. He was quite young when it happened. Things were happening in Michael's little world that we didn't know much about.

Glenda: We had different carers coming in for day shifts and night shifts when Matthew first came home. One of them liked tidiness and she used to come in and tidy up the kitchen every night. In some ways this was quite nice because it saved me from doing it but in another way it was like, 'This is our home.'

The dining room was just about big enough for Matthew. We had glass doors between there and the lounge so we used to put a blanket over it to give Matthew his privacy and then progressed to covering the glass with film to obscure it.

But there wasn't room for his wheelchair, so every night someone would wheel it into the front room to plug it in for the night, walking in front of Chris and I while we were trying to relax. But it was still so much better than having Matthew in hospital. This was our life now and compared to what Matthew had to deal with, it was nothing.

We did have some odd characters working. Sometimes you used to dread going down in the morning because if one of them had been awake all night they wanted to talk, whereas all you wanted to do was make a cup of tea and come to life.

We ended up having our breakfast in bed so we wouldn't have to engage for too long with anyone. You couldn't relax, people were around all the time.

Matthew was always going to go back to school, we never even considered him not doing so.

A special needs teacher came and saw us and we had

04.04.04

to go and see the Education Authority about what they would put in place to support him.

He wasn't really what I understood as Special Needs but had to complete an Educational Statement and I had to fill in a form. It was one of those one size fits all and didn't really cover what we were trying to do.

We had a big meeting at the school. I met Matthew there with his carers, I had rushed from work and they were late. After 20 minutes they came down and said it had all been sorted. The school had agreed to put in what Matthew needed and the authorities would fund it.

It was accepted that he'd have someone working with him on a one-to-one basis to support him when he went into school. He started back gradually. He'd had three months at home and would go back maybe two days a week at first, then gradually build it up and by the end of that term he'd be ready to do a full year.

Matthew was quite busy; he had a few social activities and went to see Sir Frank Williams a few times, the founder and team principal of the Williams Formula One racing team. He was so supportive. But one day his teacher said, 'Matthew, you're at school now these other things will have to work around it,' which was very good.

It was then he began realising that he needed to knuckle down and it was a bit more serious than popping in every now and then.

As told to David Lawrenson

14.

New Chapter

AFTER nine months in hospital confined to a life I had not chosen, I had always thought that leaving would be joyous, interspersed with feelings of relief and excitement for my future. It wasn't. It was quite simply terrifying.

I was now truly forging a new life for myself, without the safety blanket of hospital. Although nine months there had seemed like forever, it wasn't long enough to fully prepare me for what was to come but I had to move forward.

With every mile closer to home, familiar surroundings came into view again.

Entering Langford, it was as if I had never been away but I felt as if I was an intruder, an impostor in the village I had grown up in. Nothing had changed, except me.

Pulling up at home and coming through the back gate was defining. It was all down to me now and I realised it was my duty to take the reins of my future.

04.04.04

I entered the back garden and it was all there, the wooden terrace I had built with dad only months earlier, the guinea pigs, the grass.

Except now there was a large metal ramp propped up against the French doors.

The house had altered. What I had previously known to be the dining room was now filled with a hospital bed, a ventilator and hordes of equipment.

Kitchen units had been fitted to the walls to store medical supplies, a small television installed in the corner and frosted glass applied to the French doors.

It wasn't a celebration, but the gathering of family as Michael wheeled me in was symbolic. We had pulled together. We had made it.

I was pleased to be home, truly, but I was also broken, both physically and emotionally, and the strong front I felt obliged to put up came so unnaturally.

There were two support workers caring for me during the day, together with one waking night support worker and a second sleep-over carer.

My speech was still intermittent and weak, and having to instruct the support workers, whom I had only known for days, how to hoist and transfer me, undress me and put me to bed was not only tiring, but also incredibly frustrating.

In all, going to bed took over two hours. It was an indication of how difficult things were going to be.

My first trip out the following day, with us yet to source a wheelchair accessible van, was a four mile round trip to the hairdressers.

To complicate it, the powered wheelchair I had been using in hospital had been taken back before I left and as a thoroughly inadequate substitute, NHS Wheelchair Services had provided me with a cramped manual one in which I would have to be pushed everywhere.

Layered up for a December day with two rucksacks of medical equipment in tow, and Felipe, a new support worker pushing me, I took on the pavements of Langford for the first time as a wheelchair user.

Within the first couple of hundred metres of this exploratory mission, I had pothole-induced whiplash, been stuck in the middle of the main road seeking the safety of the pavement on the other side – having realised that a lowered curb on the left doesn't mean there'll be one on the right – and had stopped breathing as my ventilator pipe became entangled with the wheels.

An hour later, staring into the mirror whilst having my hair cut was the longest period I had looked at my reflection and image for a long while, but I was slowly becoming accepting of it.

Yes, I was gaunt, pale and incredibly thin but I could still see the original me inside, fighting to get back to the surface.

On the way home, in the darkness, we hit a problem.

The wheelchair could not squeeze between a wall on one side of the pavement and the curb on the other and we were forced to head into the road.

Having checked that my arms and feet were secure on the wheelchair and waited for a break in the traffic, Felipe dipped the front wheels into the road, straightened the chair up, and ran. The fact that the cars had slowed did not seem to dent his enthusiasm and, as we reached the curb back onto the pavement, he slowed not a bit.

The subsequent jolt was accompanied by an

unfathomable crack which I was sure was my bones, but seconds later the distinct tilt in the wheelchair's balance gave us the answer. He had only gone and knocked the bloody front wheel off.

Christmas Eve 2004, a week later, was a world away from how I'd previously spent it but what I did have was my new chin-operated, powered wheelchair.

It cost £25,000, which was out of reach for the NHS and I was incredibly grateful to charities who helped fund it, especially the children's charity, Variety.

Opening my eyes the following morning, my head screamed with pain I had never before experienced, nor believed possible. I could not shout loud enough, nor do anything but be consumed by the seeming explosions going off in my brain.

Through blurred vision brought on by my tears, I was suddenly aware of mum's presence as she removed my blocked catheter.

The backup of urine in my bladder had triggered something I had heard so very much about in Stoke Mandeville, but which up until that point I had not experienced: autonomic dysreflexia.

Although I could no longer physically feel pain in any region below my level of injury, my body still reacts to it through increasing blood pressure until the source is identified and removed.

Had mum not been a nurse, that episode of AD would most likely have led to a stroke or worse. As a result, Christmas Day was not entirely pleasant, but I did manage to unwrap my presents, with Michael's assistance, by pulling the wrapping off with my teeth, until I got a paper cut on my lip.

The days and weeks which followed passed in a blur of excitement, trepidation, fear, and more than anything, frustration at the limitations now enforced upon me.

Time without any means of exploring the world beyond the confines of Langford, was becoming claustrophobic in the extreme.

Now that I was home, I no longer had a goal or challenge to fight for each day and I could feel myself stagnating and becoming lonelier with each passing day.

The only saving grace were my painting classes.

Painting had never been a forte of mine but was something forced on me by the occupational therapists in Stoke Mandeville.

They fashioned a mouth stick which I would hold between my teeth with the aim of strengthening my neck muscles, and to which could be attached a pen or paintbrush.

I started by mastering writing my name and quickly progressed to tracing pictures and thereafter putting paint to paper.

My first attempts were painting by numbers but soon I was creating crude landscapes, and having something tangible which I had produced and could look at was huge for my morale.

Returning home, it wasn't long before grandma enlisted the help of one of her long-standing friends, Josie – a wonderful lady with great artistic flair – to assist with my painting.

She would mix the paints and starting with a tree, a field and then a fence, I slowly built my repertoire and confidence much to her joy and encouragement.

Painting quickly became the crux around which I could give meaning and structure to my days.

04.04.04

As I became more confident, I would dabble by myself and look forward to showing Josie the fruits of my labour. I began painting pictures to say thank you to those that had stuck by me through the turbulent times.

Subsequently, many have been sold for charity, whilst others have been blown up into Christmas cards to raise money for the Rugby Football League Benevolent Fund.

The on-going hunt for an adequate wheelchair accessible vehicle, however, had proved fruitless.

They were either not high enough, long enough or didn't have space to accommodate all our family, plus the constant presence of my two support workers.

The search was dad's baby and he was determined not to compromise.

Of all the places, ebay provided the solution. A 20-year-old bright blue Renault Master van, equipped with a hydraulic wheelchair lift, came up for auction and looked to be the perfect short-term solution. We were soon the owners of this un-loved, beaten up, rusted old saviour, which to me was the key to unlock my future.

Up to this point, it was easy for me to talk a good game and express my desire to return to school, watch a game of rugby or simply go out to the pub, but now I had the means to do so, and there was nothing to stop me.

The weeks that followed were a tentative entry into the world of unrestricted freedom. It was the first time since my accident that I had both the control, and the option, to do what I wanted, when I wanted.

I started by attempting simple everyday tasks; going shopping, watching Michael play football and, more frequently, going to the cinema. There, I could quietly sit alone and escape the daily barrage of challenges and fears.

THROUGHOUT this whole experience, right from my first moments waking up in Leeds there was one thing which we, as a family, had promised ourselves; a dog.

Mum and dad sat around my hospital bed in Intensive Care and promised that not only would I be home before Christmas but we would get ourselves a pooch.

We had friends who owned labradors, and had seen programmes on TV showing them helping those with disabilities, so it was the obvious choice.

The following February, we visited kennels just a few minutes' drive up the road. The owner held the puppies close to my face so I could move my head and feel their fur on my skin.

All squirmed except a golden one who placed her paws on me and snuggled her head into the gap between my neck and shoulder. She had chosen me.

Nugget was an immediate hit, charming in every single way and it was beautiful to feel the softness of her fur.

When taking her for walks we would tie her lead to my wheelchair and I adored the connection that built between us; having Nugget as company during the day brought endless happiness and laughs.

That is until one morning in March 2005. In my dazed state as I woke up, I was sure I could hear screaming.

Dad came running into my room crying, almost hysterically. 'It's Nugget, she's dead! I'm so sorry. Matthew,' he said leaning over the bed and cradling my head, tears now streaming down both of our faces.

'What have we done so wrong? What have we done to deserve this?' dad kept repeating.

04.04.04

He blamed himself. As he was going out the back gate on his way to work, Nugget had bolted for the gap, ran out into the road, was hit by a car and killed almost instantly. The screams I heard were dad's as all this played out in front of his eyes.

It had been a turbulent year, one which in our worst nightmares we couldn't have envisaged but this truly was the darkness before dawn.

15.
School Life

16 March 2005 was the day I feared would never come, it was the date I returned to school.

Understandably, going to bed the night before I had butterflies in my stomach and felt sick to the core with nerves; I knew much of what to expect but not how and if I would cope. I would confront places, people and situations I was scared of.

Waking early, the usual morning routine ablutions dragged on but I could not be late. This was the first day of rebuilding my life.

The angst built as 8am came and went and, in the rush, I'd not given my body enough time to readjust and acclimatise for the drop in blood pressure which I knew would come with sitting in my wheelchair.

I had fallen back into the mindset of a young, fit, Matthew King and overlooked, or more likely, ignored, every warning sign my body told me.

04.04.04

Transferring from bed, blood drained from my head into my feet and I fainted. Needless to say, my first day back at school was delayed 24 hours.

This time I was in situ an hour earlier, eased my way into the day and was eventually heading towards Stratton Upper School, retracing a journey I had last taken 11 months earlier.

Arriving in the school car park, there were no spaces. Even the two disabled bays were full, and as the van sat waiting, hordes of pupils were forced to go around us, their attention automatically driven to the large wheelchair sat in the back.

The familiar unease I felt in such situations was overpowering.

We found a spot near the bus stop and I made my way into the school through the disabled entrance I had never previously even noticed was there.

Waiting in the lobby for Miss Harper, my geography teacher and the head of sixth form, the dreaded sound of the school bell signalled the impending flood of students exiting registration and heading to the first lesson.

My response was impulsive and automatic. I pushed up on the joystick, engaged the motors on my wheelchair, and moved to the safety and obscurity of the corner where I was passed without a second look. In my heart, I knew this couldn't go on and the time would soon come when I would have no choice but to face up to everybody.

Miss Harper was a comforting face, someone who had recognised the warning signs of my potential educational derailment a couple of years earlier.

She brought the very best out of me when studying for my GCSEs and I respected her enormously.

As we moved down the corridor, nothing had changed, yet I was now seeing everything from a very different perspective. No longer the six foot teenager dominating my surroundings but now looking up at everything and everyone.

Entering the sixth form, many of the faces were familiar and had come to visit me in Stoke Mandeville. These were my friends, my peers, the people I was most afraid of being presented to in my new form.

I can only imagine how utterly different I must have looked to them; I was now seven stone in weight, anaemic and just the shell of the boy I had been but, if they did have the desire to stare, they didn't show it.

Gathering around me, first in a trickle and then in more of a constant tide of faces and voices, if I had been in any doubt that I would be welcomed back unreservedly, I was soon left in none.

Sitting my AS-Levels before my accident, I was studying Geography, History, English Literature, and Biology, but because of the various consequences and practicalities associated with my condition, it was abundantly clear that it wouldn't be possible to pick up where I had left off.

Firstly, there were my fatigue levels. At this point, I was prone to succumbing to sleep at any time of the day and couldn't hold my concentration for any significant period.

Medication and the physical toll that re-engaging in everyday life was having on me was draining my emaciated body of every spare kilojoule of energy. Four subjects was off the cards.

Sara Cain of Connexions – an educational advice facility – had been the catalyst for my return to school.

During my discussions with her in hospital, it became

obvious how limited my future employment options now were and I had to focus on careers that only required mental and intellectual input.

Any career would need a stable base, a warm office and a door I could shut when having medical procedures carried out. Law had become the front runner.

Surrounded by my friends, Mrs Duncan, the Head of Special Needs at Stratton, reminded me I had work to do.

She was fairly robust in her approach to me and her forthright attitude was refreshing. She wasn't mollycoddling or pampering me, but rather treating me as she did any of her other students, and I immediately respected her for that.

I did a test GCSE Geography question with her to assess my capability. Fumbling with instructions and descriptions, I was struck by the difficulty of expressing myself in a way that others could understand and relate to.

It was exasperating work but I wasn't overly disheartened.

At that time, in order to secure a place for university, it was necessary to attain a certain number of UCAS points and I resolved that if I achieved good grades in two subjects that would prove my intellectual ability.

History and Geography were the ones I pinned my future on and leaving school that day I felt a profound sense of relief that some tangible route was now becoming clear.

The visits into school that followed were more of a bedding-in process. In discussions with the teachers, it was decided that I would start back full-time when the new school year began in September and so each trip thereafter was intended to ensure that I would be able to hit the ground running when the time came.

The most important development during these

months before the school holidays was the introduction to my two scribes who were to act as my hands and assist me with anything physical I could no longer perform: turning pages, highlighting textbooks, writing down my dictated notes and answers, and giving me a nudge to wake me during lessons.

Pam had been working in the special needs department at Stratton for a number of years and the school recruited an additional employee, Judy, as my scribe for the remainder of my studies.

In order to cut down any work I would have to do on my own at home, we spent the free periods together reviewing the notes they had made during the lessons so they were in a format I was happy with.

It was invaluable preparation and, more than anything, it gave us a chance to get to know each other.

There were still obstacles, though. One July morning, as I was in the drawn out process of being lowered to the floor by the wheelchair lift in the van, I could see a group of six or seven students looking out the window and intently watching my exit.

Amongst the group, the young boy standing in the middle was pointing me out to his friends and giggling hysterically, which they quickly joined in with. I was a laughing stock.

That moment destroyed me. I found myself at a crossroads.

Still incredibly self-conscious, the easy option as I looked to the ground hoping it would swallow me up, would have been to get back in the van, go home and forget any school future.

I chose instead to confront the situation head on.

I knew who I was and still retained the same stubbornness, resolve and strength I had always possessed and so, when heading to history that afternoon, I took matters into my own hands.

No longer did I divert my gaze from those looking at me, but defiantly returned their stares. My instincts had taken over and all I had to do was follow them.

I'd won a personal battle of mind over matter.

Returning after the long summer break, I was eager to make an instant impression.

Moving through the school, rather than having an almost constant feeling of being judged by the students, it now felt as if they were comfortable with me.

No longer were there stares coming at me from all directions but gestures of kindness and understanding, not just from my immediate group of friends and acquaintances, but from students of all year groups.

Opening doors for me, corralling their friends out of my path in the corridor, a nod of recognition; the smallest things were making the biggest difference.

What was still difficult, though, was that it simply wasn't within the unconfident me to approach a clique of friends and attempt to build new relationships.

My cousin Sarah took me under her wing which, with my contemporaries having moved on to university, helped avoid the awkwardness of sitting in the common room by myself.

The process of dictating my work as opposed to scribbling down the words with pen and paper was a huge learning curve and one which was at first difficult to get to grips with.

My mind was working at a far faster pace than Pam's

pen and so the constant review of what I'd said and where the essay was going, began to ingrain itself as a fundamental trait.

School was slowly becoming second nature. With temperatures dropping as winter drew in, a fan heater found its way on to the desk in my side room.

Turning it on was the first task every day with no thought as to whether it was cooking Pam, Judy or an increasing stream of passing friends.

I had my comeuppance when leaving my hand trailing in front of it for an hour whilst Pam and I were going over Hitler's seeming unstoppable rise to power.

Pam began packing away our materials and when she pressed the power button on the wheelchair to allow me to back away from the desk, I looked down at my left hand and saw the devastation that had been caused.

With my lack of sensation leaving me unable to feel the build up of heat on my skin, inch-long heat blisters were inflicted on the outside of each of my forefingers.

It was the most grotesque feeling to know that I had caused so much injury to myself but yet been completely unaware of doing so.

The subsequent weeks, during which each of my fingers were bathed in iodine and bandaged, proved to be an enduring lesson, one which has left me overly cautious to the risk of potential damage.

Christmas 2005 was another momentous landmark.

In the year since my return home, the cramped dining room had remained my quasi-bedroom.

Ever since my arrival, architects plans had been drawn up, revised, and then finalised for an annex to be built from the rear of the house.

It was intended as my new bedroom and the one area I could call my own. Building work had been started in the autumn and their hard work paid off with the room ready for me to move into on Christmas Eve – boy, was it perfect.

The extension was twice as big as the dining room. There was light coming in from every direction, and dad's company had designed furniture which allowed me, from my lowered viewpoint in my wheelchair, to see in every cupboard, look in each drawer and have complete control.

A specially designed desk had been installed in the corner of the room which allowed my wheelchair to slide underneath, giving me access to a stable surface for my laptop, painting materials and textbooks.

It was an immediate improvement for us all at home and day-to-day life was no longer full of compromises.

As the weeks passed, it was comforting to be able to assess my life in terms of coursework deadlines and exams, as opposed to therapies and operations.

With the exam season on me, I was as well prepared as I could be as I headed into the designated side room with Pam to dictate my answers.

For the first, Mrs Duncan had designated herself as the invigilator which added a layer of tension in the confined space but exams had never phased me and off I went into a detailed description of the events of Omaha beach on D-Day.

I cut short a planned ten minute break so as not to lose my sense of flow and ploughed on but, as the end neared, hot flushes on my face and Pam's confirmation of my red complexion confirmed my worst fears; autonomic dysreflexia.

It was the inextricably awful physical consequence of the blocked catheter I'd experienced when I'd first left hospital and meant that I had to get home, and quickly.

Dictating the conclusion as swiftly as Pam could write, my vision was failing me by the time the final full stop had been written.

Not stopping to proof read the essay, as soon as I was happy I could conjure no more I called my support workers and told them to put their foot down. Getting home, I was in a state of utter panic.

The headache which had exploded on Christmas Day was creeping up on me like an unstoppable tsunami and, once transferred to bed, the search for whatever was causing my body to suffer began.

My face and chest were blotchy and clammy to touch and I began to struggle to breathe; a panic attack.

The removal of my jeans immediately exposed the source of the problem. The bag strapped to my leg which collected my urine was completely empty and given that it hadn't been checked since first thing that morning, something was not right.

There was clearly a huge discrepancy between the water I had drunk and the amount of urine my body had produced.

I understood that if I didn't insert a new catheter immediately, my body would begin to fail me. Knowing that mum was too far away at work to help, the only way out was to compose myself and rationally explain to Roger, my support worker, what needed to be done.

As he began preparing my catheter, he noticed that the flip-flow valve which, when pointing downwards allowed the urine to drain, was turned upwards and had been for the past nine hours.

Reversing the valve, both urine and some blood flowed immediately. Clearly, the adrenaline that I'd produced when concentrating so earnestly for the exam had dulled all other responses, holding off the onset of attack.

With every passing minute the blood became more diluted and relief set in.

That wasn't the way I had intended to complete the exam but my body had held out just about long enough to suppress every biological symptom to allow me to do what needed to be done.

Whereas in hospital I had begun to see my body as a foreign object and one which had failed me on so many occasions, that day proved that the same spirit I had always prided myself on was still present.

Two weeks of exams followed uneventfully and leaving school for the final time on 18 June, I was content that nothing more could have been done.

When the results were released, I had achieved an A grade in both subjects. I had got to the point where I was being assessed on a par with my peers, with no sympathy or preferential treatment.

Now, I was only looking to the future.

16.

Swedish Slopes

IT was whilst sitting down with Josie at my improvised painting desk, in the heat of summer, that my journey to the ski slopes of Sweden, began.

When attempting my first snowy landscape, a Backup Trust pamphlet was pushed through the letterbox.

That was the charity nurse Tracey had told me about whilst I was in hospital and ever since I had harboured the desire to push the limits of what was achievable.

The back page listed the dates for upcoming courses and events and my eye stopped on 6 October 2005, 'Ski Taster Day, Bracknell Dry Ski Slope.'

I enquired about the possibility of attending and whilst they had never had a participant with such a high level of injury, in theory, there were no glaring reasons why I should not go along to see whether it was possible.

In the following six weeks or so, this exciting prospect

glowed like a burning ember in the back of my mind. My respiratory needs were the crunch point.

Sitting in the ski cart, I would be away from everybody who could look after my ventilator and would have no way of signalling to get help should the pipe become detached. I would be taking a huge risk.

Nevertheless, with everything that had transpired in the past 18 months or so, I was determined to embrace every opportunity.

Arriving at the ski slope, I was soon being whisked along in the organisers' slipstream as we made our way to the holding area at the bottom to be greeted by a bizarre looking contraption which at first sight resembled a primitive bobsleigh.

The cart was a blue plastic shell, attached to which were skis on each of the four corners with poles linked to the front two steering ones.

As my doubts surfaced, a giant adrenaline-junkie knelt beside me and introduced himself as Nick, the chap in whose hands I would be placing my life.

He told me his history as a spinal physiotherapist at Stoke Mandeville who had many years' experience caring for patients in hospital on ventilators and was fully proficient in every aspect of my medical care.

Four strong guys then came over and lifted me from my wheelchair into the cart and I was now sitting barely 15 centimetres off the ground.

Simply being so close was a beautifully reassuring feeling; seeing the ground up close was something I had missed and, strangely, all my fears dissipated and I felt an emotion I had not experienced in an awful long time – sheer unbridled excitement.

In order to stop my body escaping the cart at the first sign of a bump or an overly aggressive carving of a turn, my legs and feet were secured with rope, hands strapped across my body with Velcro straps, my ventilator tubing was taped to my chest with gaffer tape and the vent strapped to the front of my legs.

I was being used as a human guinea pig which was bizarrely refreshing.

Nick gave me one last get out of jail free card saying, 'Matt, you ready for the ride of your life?' but he could already tell the answer from my beaming grin.

From the ski lift, I could see dad looking on with a mixture of pride and utter terror, and the ever-increasing cheers of encouragement coming from the organisers, other participants and fellow skiers made me truly feel a million dollars.

I could only equate it to the sensation I used to get when running out of the changing room onto the rugby pitch before a big game.

Up on the slope, Nick used the two poles attached to my front skis to steer the cart towards the centre of the run, they passed over the top lip and it succumbed to the ever-increasing pull of gravity.

There wasn't an ounce of fear in me as we built up speed and started to slalom from left to right across the slope.

Sitting so close to the ground, feeling the air hit my face and moving along the surface at an ever increasing speed was so exhilarating.

Coming to a halt at the bottom, the excitement inside me was mirrored by the grin spread across dad's face. 'Surely you can go quicker than that!' he queried, laughing.

And quicker we went. I didn't want to mess about

with all the slaloms, I just wanted to smash the slope and hear the wind hiss as it passed my ears at an ever increasing velocity.

In those dark days in hospital where life seemed so devoid of anything good or rewarding, I never imagined anything like this was possible.

But here I was and those minutes on the slope woke something inside me which had lay dormant since those fateful minutes on the pitch a seeming lifetime ago.

In the weeks that followed, preparations began in earnest for Sweden.

Not only had nobody ever attempted skiing on a ventilator, there was also the not insignificant obstacle of flying with my 180 kg electric wheelchair, five boxes of medical equipment and a portable hoist.

On more than one occasion it became apparent that I had perhaps bitten off more than I could chew.

As I had found out to my detriment in Stoke Mandeville, when I become cold there is little I can do to warm up again and so travelling to -20° degree temperatures clearly wasn't ideal.

Stockings, winter socks, ski boots, thermals, tracksuit bottoms, yet more thermals, woollen jumpers, more thermals, two woolly hats, gloves, some strange contraption called an 'octopus system' which would blow warm air into my clothes, yet more thermals and a hot water bottle, were all assembled.

My medical equipment filling two cars, I set off to Heathrow, concerned about the effects of the pressurised cabin on my ventilator and a first coach journey at the other side, never mind the mountains.

The skiing party, including support workers and

volunteers, met for dinner in an airport hotel the night before the flight after which I skulked away to my room and began a sleepless night of endless self-doubts.

Early the next day, six wheelchairs and 22 people checked in. As our flight was called a number of gentleman wearing high visibility jackets approached and we were transferred into aisle chairs, from which, on board, we would be lifted into our seats.

As the plane left the runway, so did my lingering worries and fatigue overcame me. Despite my determination to stay awake and embrace the experience, my next recollection was waking just in time for us to land at Åre Östersund Airport.

Reunited with our luggage, we set off and instantly the cold at dusk hit me.

We survived a hair-raising transfer to the hotel, our driver showing little concern for the snow and ice. Going to bed, I was like a child on Christmas morning. I couldn't wait to be out on the slopes.

Arriving at the ski school, we were met by six carts aligned next to one another. I was the last of our group to transfer into mine because of the ventilator – I was to be a pioneer.

One by one, I watched the others head off into the snow and with each passing minute my anticipation grew.

Attached to the roof of the ski school was a hoist similar to the medical one in hospital and I was lifted and transferred across into the cart

Nick was working there for the whole winter season and building on our experience at Bracknell it didn't take long to cobble together a failsafe system to keep my legs, arms and ventilator safe.

Duct tape strapping my helmet to the roll cage of the ski cart to protect my neck muscles was the last procedure and we were off.

The first thing to hit me was the silence. The serenity of skiing over freshly fallen snow was hypnotising.

Reaching the ski lift, we bypassed the long queue and were the first to take the journey up the mountain; I was beginning to learn that queue jumping was one of the unforeseen silver linings of a spinal-cord injury.

Coming off the lift half way up a slalom course, we were off.

Approaching the first flag, I naïvely thought that Nick would take it easy and guide us around it at a safe distance.

He didn't, we clipped it with the side of the cart and then immediately cut a sharp turn into the snow and headed back at 90 degrees towards the next one.

Speed, thrill and exhilaration best sum up the hours and days that followed.

With each subsequent trip we would leave the lift one further stop up, giving more time and space to explore the mountain and exactly where each of our respective limits for pushing boundaries actually was.

On our first red run, we were joined by Oleg, another ski instructor from the same school. Clearly, this was a fairly momentous moment, not just in my life but for the school and so he followed us down and recorded what ensued.

Sitting at the top of the run, it was a moment I instinctively knew I would remember forever. I was 18 years old, paralysed from the neck down, strapped into a ski cart in a 'that'll do' kind of a way, with a crazed instructor behind me shouting, 'Everything is going to be okay... Dude!'

Metaphorically speaking, it felt as if I was throwing

myself off a mountain with no parachute. Literally speaking, ditto.

We crested the top of the run and the immediate pull of gravity was just ridiculous. Whilst Nick traversed the slope from side to side and in doing so scrubbed off much of our speed, every time we straightened up, we took off.

The run was one of the longest and most treacherous at the resort, with rocks and trees bordering both sides, and the gradient peaked and troughed until finally the horizon opened out.

Halfway down, the visual blur of an attack on my senses was replaced by an acute pain.

The ski cart hit an undulation in the snow, catapulting us into the air for what I recall was an eternity, but which, in reality, was probably a small hop.

As we came down and hit the surface, the whole cart was rocked and my head thrown forward by the impact.

That would have been fine, had it not been for the fact that my helmet was secured to the roll cage, and therefore immovable.

Although the majority of my head remained strapped into the helmet, my forehead had been forced forward and was now exposed to the freezing temperature and 30 mile per hour wind chill.

I suffered brain freeze which intensified with every second, and by the time we came to a stop at the bottom of the slope I was able to focus on nothing else.

Oleg's filming had him coming to a halt next to me in clouds of snow, beaming and claiming, 'Holy crap, that was fast!' A drink was most definitely now called for.

And après-ski we certainly did, squeezing my way self-consciously through a thronged dance floor at the chosen, packed pub to my first beer, which was already sitting there waiting for me.

There was quickly a second Jägermeister, a third followed by a tequila and then a fourth, I reckon, by which time I was pretty much battered.

The photographs that night continue to tell the story of flaming Sambucas dripping down my front, a session on the microphone with the band and, even with my limited movement, the invention of a slightly weird head-banging type dance move, all of which I scarcely remember.

But it was good to be back!

Aside from the once-in-a-lifetime skiing experiences, that achievement of simply going out and enjoying myself, dancing, partying and drinking, was one of the major positives I took away from Sweden.

I now felt completely healed of the mental wounds inflicted since 04.04.04.

17.

Cap and Gown

AS with most students, the summer after my A-level results was spent mainly lazing around but I did use the time to kick start my university career.

Uni had been my horizon for a good while and whilst I had contemplated faraway seats of learning, it had fairly quickly dawned on me that, with my care needs, the only realistic options would be establishments within a commutable distance of home.

In short, my choice was between the University of Bedfordshire and the University of Hertfordshire and I went for the latter.

Before I opened the envelope which confirmed my grades, I had travelled there and met with the Faculty of Law's head of admissions to discuss my prospects of being accepted. With the grades achieved, as of 1st October I was a university student.

Freshers week passed me by and as much as I longed to get involved and integrate myself with my fellow students, the intimidation brought on by seeing them going about the registration process in groups meant I was simply unable to start off on the right foot.

Entering the library in the main university campus, having had my photo taken for the ID badge, I was then whisked away by one of the lecturers overseeing the whole process to a computer tucked away in the corner, completed the online registration, and then headed off to the Law School which was located some five miles away in St Albans.

The disabled entrance at the back of the lecture theatre through which I entered the building was blocked by a horde of boxes.

Waiting unceremoniously outside in the cold for the caretaker to arrive, I watched as 11 o'clock came and went and with it the start of the first lecture introducing the course.

Once finally able to get into the building, my conspicuous entrance was completed by having to pass across the front of the theatre to the designated wheelchair space on the far side. To say my start to university life had been less than ideal was an understatement.

For the remainder of the week I had introductory lectures on each core topic I would be studying that year but found myself coming out of the theatre feeling more and more out of my depth, the legal jargon being thrown around by the lecturers was utterly intimidating,

In the silence of the auditorium, aside from the lecturer's voice, the constant noise of which I was so conscious was the wheezing of my ventilator as it sucked in and drew the air from my lungs. It was completely unsettling.

Each lecture was followed by squeezing myself into

the lift and heading upstairs to the Learning Resource Centre. It was tiny and the only way to fit inside was to take my feet off of the foot plates on my wheelchair and carefully manipulate them to the sides of the lift.

The LRC was the place where I chose to spend much of my time completing the compulsory reading and working on the tasks for the seminars.

It was also the place where, in that first week, I had fundamental doubts as to whether this was for me.

I found that only studying two A-levels had left me hugely undercooked for what was to come at degree level.

The amount of reading was overwhelming, and I began panicking that once again, I had overestimated my capabilities.

On the Friday, I found myself working with Pam in one of the empty classrooms of the law school, and simply broke down.

University life was not what I had hoped it would be and for the first time I found myself intellectually swamped.

I went to bed that night resigned to giving it up but I couldn't sleep and, in the early hours, called Felipe in to my bedroom, asked for the lights to be turned on, my reading stand placed on my bed in front of me, and my contract law textbook opened at chapter one, page one.

With him wielding a yellow highlighter and marking the passages I identified, by the time dawn broke on Saturday morning I had completed the compulsory reading for Monday's seminar, but more importantly, crossed an all-important line.

The previous evening I was defeated.

There were so many excuses I could use to rationalise my seeming failure but that night, by simply getting my head down and working hard, I had brought my future back under my control.

That little success reignited something else which was ingrained and had been partially hidden since the accident; all my life I don't recall ever giving up or putting in anything other than my best.

That was not about to change now.

From that day on, I vowed to myself I would never leave myself unprepared and in the months that followed, I slowly found myself becoming accustomed to academic life, although sleep became my nemesis.

Sitting in the front row of the theatre with the lectern just metres to my right and the PowerPoint slides projected onto the huge screen in front of me, near-unconsciousness often crept up on me.

The contorted look on my face as I sought to suppress the first yawn, the wiggling of my jaw in the hope that movement would awaken me, repeated blinking of my eyes; they were my only defences, and they failed lecture after lecture, day after day.

There was, however, one rather unwelcome nuance of my condition which never failed to indicate my presence in the near-silent auditorium and that was my bowels or, more specifically, a build of gas that I could do nothing about.

Sitting on a rubber cushion in the wheelchair only served to emphasise the eventual rumble and I was frequently distinctly aware that I was about to release an epic fart and have the eyes of every student and most probably the lecturer, on me.

Sometimes, in those vital seconds preceding, I would cunningly ask a question of Pam or begin dictating a note for her to record, thinking that if I talked and distracted myself, surely everybody else wouldn't notice.

As we began working towards our exams, I spent the Easter holidays and all of April, May and June with little else for company other than my textbooks and lecture notes.

But it all paid off, the hours of sacrifice spent in the run-up meant that I came out of each exam knowing I had nailed it.

In each of the four core subjects I received a distinction and to top it all, the award for the highest grades of any first year law student by the exam board.

I had come unrecognisably far from that first week when I thought of packing it all in.

What I lacked in ability I more than made up for in honest grit and determination and continued in that vein over the next two years of study which also included work placements in various law firms and court rooms and even a stint in Parliament.

Once again, I topped the results list for the second year with my newfound love for the law. My confidence was at an all-time high, and I was seemingly on my way to a first class honours degree.

My finals comprised of four modules; Company Law, Employment Law, Equity and Trusts, and Environmental Law, with three days between each of the exams.

The first exam went according to plan. Not even feeling nervous, the shock was when turning up for the second ready and primed for Employment Law, my favourite subject, only to have the paper turned over to find that I was being tested on Equity and Trusts, the hardest one to master.

And with that, the bottom fell out of my world.

Despite all my preparation, in the seconds which

followed the gut-wrenching, nauseating, hideous reality hit me that I had revised and turned up for the wrong exam.

As Pam sat down, the look on my face gave me away as unbridled alarm set in.

What followed were three of the most uncomfortable and nerve-shredding hours imaginable.

Fumbling around for statutes and cases to back up my answers, I mumbled on saying 10 words, where five would have done.

It was a disaster, three years of hard work wrecked, it was my fault, and I had nobody to blame but myself.

But I still had two exams to finish and if I was to salvage anything from my time in university, they had to be the best to papers I ever sat.

They were, but passing out of that same fire exit which three years earlier I had sat outside in the cold waiting to be allowed in, I saw myself as a failure, capable of so much more.

Whenever waiting for results, whether at school or university, I was always nervous more with excitement than trepidation. This time, I was dreading it.

On the back of my previous university results, I had been invited to the Hertfordshire Law Society's annual summer dinner at Hatfield House.

I felt something of a fraud sitting amongst my lecturers, tutors and the highest ranks of Hertfordshire's legal profession knowing that I had stuffed up when it mattered most.

With mum and dad sat beside me, it was almost adding insult to injury to hear about how much of a model student I had been.

Then, as Klearchos Kyriakides, a tutor I respected

greatly, began what I thought would be more small talk, the smallest slip of his tongue filled me with hope.

'Matt, I know it's not official yet, but congratulations!' he said.

'What?' I replied, shocked, 'You know the results already?'

He responded, 'Just taken a quick look. Your name's at the top of the list.'

Quite how I did it, I don't know, but I had scraped a first class honours degree, one of only five in the year.

The crowning moment was the graduation ceremony, I had exceeded everybody's expectations, not least my own.

Driving up the ramp onto the stage at St Albans Cathedral to receive my certificate, with the backdrop of cheers from my friends, was undoubtedly the proudest moment of my life.

18.
Marathon Effort

AT the core of everything I was achieving was support from so many people, and at the heart of that was the ever-strengthening bond between myself and Chris Hawkins.

He continued to subject himself to gruelling physical challenges and we were now pretty much speaking every day, plotting ways to push the limits of what I could achieve.

We were thick as thieves.

On the back of our friendship – and the apparent lack of support for those injured playing rugby league – Chris and his partner Lesley formed XIII Heroes, a charity whose objective was to financially assist those in such need.

In the years since my discharge, the charity had organised all manner of events but it also spawned one of the greatest challenges of my life.

At the stage where I now considered myself to be back leading a normal day-to-day life, it felt almost unjust simply sitting back and accepting support; now I wanted to give something back.

I had gone along and watched others undertake marathons, parachute jumps, long distance treks and the like, but as I sat there, something was yearning inside me; a desire to accomplish in my own right, to be in the vanguard, pushing the limits of possibility.

I no longer wanted to be the honorary mascot and so, after much discussion and negotiation, I embarked upon training for and completing the 2006 BUPA Great North Run.

I crossed the line in two hours, 58 minutes and in doing so achieved a world first for somebody with my level of disability.

The exertion of having to hold my head upright and control the wheelchair for 13 miles had been exceptionally gruelling but, as I made the finish, I knew I could do more.

For me, the natural progression was to compete in my home marathon in London, but it was not to be.

Despite finishing the GNR, run under the same rules and regulations as those governing the London Marathon, the powers that be were having none of it.

Various rebuttals and defences came back to each of my applications, mainly centring on the fact that my powered wheelchair would breach the rules and give me a 'competitive advantage'.

It was infuriating that they had lost sight of the whole purpose of the event; for the majority of the runners taking part each year, it is a personal challenge at an occasion which brings mankind together and shows what is possible and, for me, it was no different.

I simply could not fathom that my paralysis could be considered an 'advantage', and after much to-ing and fro-ing,

the real reason why the organisers did not want me to take part became clear when I received what seemed a definitive reply.

'The London Marathon is an event of athletic endeavour and although Mr King's efforts in driving his wheelchair over such an extended period may be thought admirable, it cannot be said to be athletic endeavour without mechanical aids. [Declining Mr King's application] is important not merely because of the image that we wish to project but because of the rules of our sport under which the event is held and sanctioned.'

This letter was signed by Nick Bitel, at that time the chief executive of the London Marathon who went on to become chair of Sport England.

Never beforehand had I considered that simply allowing a man to participate in a powered wheelchair was capable of damaging the 'image' of an event, but perhaps I was wrong.

With London, ridiculously, off the agenda, the New York Marathon was the next alternative and after tentative discussions and an explanation of my situation, it soon became apparent that the organisers do have discretion as to who they allow to compete, and they could not have been more open or accommodating.

Chris secured a place not just for me but also a team of five runners to compete on behalf of the Christopher and Dana Reeve Foundation, the charity established by the late *Superman* actor to fund pioneering research aimed at identifying a cure for spinal cord injury.

With my need for medical support around the entire route, the organisers even permitted two medically-trained cyclists to follow me; so mum and dad stepped up.

With the arrangements sorted, all that was left were the not so minor tasks of training, organising the trip to New York and, of course, funding it.

Very soon after having secured my place in the 2007 event, we approached the Anglo Irish Bank with a view to them sponsoring at least part of the considerable cost in attempting this world first.

Much to mine and Chris's delight, in return for having their corporate logo emblazoned across our chests, they agreed to cover the entire amount.

My first venture onto the roads that March saw me drive the wheelchair from my home in Langford, the five miles to my uncle's house in a nearby village, and back again.

With my support workers driving my car on the road behind me, we made the journey at a steady pace of four-and-a-half miles per hour and in doing so incurred the wrath of many out for a Sunday morning drive.

The blaring horns, not so pleasant hand gestures and even a driver slowing down to give me a mouthful for obstructing the highway left me in no doubt that I needed to find an alternative way to train.

Eventually, I was offered the exclusive use of Bedford Autodrome, a corporate track circuit run by Motorsport Vision on the outskirts of town.

Closed on Sundays, it was entirely mine to drive around in the wheelchair for as many miles as my neck could handle and in the months to follow I spent many a happy hour pounding around the track with music blaring in my ears and, for the most part, the sun on my face.

As soon as Chris and I made this crazy adventure public, we were inundated with willing volunteers and very quickly our team was complete: Paul O'Brien, Gina Goldrick,

Helen Goldthorpe, Laura Harrison and Craig Drake joined us for this incredible adventure.

In anticipation of the ordeals my body was likely to undergo, I spent the day before we left in bed and, following a sleepless night of anticipation, we made it to Heathrow for a photoshoot with the sponsors.

We were also joined by Matt James, an engineer from the wheelchair manufacturer, to ensure it did not fail me on the way round the course.

The long flight to JFK turned out to be a feat of endurance in itself. My height meant that for the entire seven hour flight my head was far above the top of the seat and therefore completely unsupported.

My body, so used to being positioned upright in the wheelchair, didn't take kindly to being slouched and so left me with surges of high blood pressure as the dreaded autonomic dysreflexia repeatedly came at me in waves, hardly the ideal preparation.

That was nothing compared to when Matt came back with the wheelchair, post disembarkation. He was apoplectic. The baggage handlers had managed to drop it from the conveyor belt as they were offloading it from the plane and it was mangled.

The headrest and chin control were bent out of all recognition, the plastic casing protecting the electronics was smashed, and there was a disconcerting amount of unwanted movement in the joint connecting the backrest to the seat.

With a hammer, Matt set about putting the chair back together and, although it wasn't perfect and there were some unwelcome creaks and groans as I made my way from the departure hall and out into a cold, winter New York night, I was still in the game.

Our team arrived there two days before the marathon, giving us all time to counteract the jetlag and take in some of the sights of this amazing city.

We were staying just a few blocks from Central Park and a short walk to Times Square, and so I became fairly accustomed to the uneven sidewalks and the lack of dropped curbs, but the Big Apple just blew me away.

Taking part as 'Team Reeve' meant attending the pre-event publicity functions and I was fortunate to meet Christopher's family; representing their charity brought with it validation of everything I had achieved.

Come the start, I wrapped up as I had done in Sweden and, passing through the foyer of the hotel, all my family were there to see me off. This was as big a moment for them as it was for me.

There was a designated bus allocated to take the wheelchair participants from Manhattan to the holding area at the start line and even jumping on at 6am I could already feel the electricity and palpable excitement. I was incredibly pumped up.

Crossing the line, I recall thinking back to my first meeting with Chris years earlier when I was a patient and he was the athlete. We were now equals, attempting this feat as teammates and friends.

I was completely overwhelmed and awestruck by the view creeping up around me as we neared the crest of the Verrazano Bridge.

With the Manhattan skyline to my left and the world opening up in front of me, it truly was a memorable moment and I would have been in a state of utter contentment had it not been for the worrying warnings emanating from the wheelchair controller.

Looking down to my left, I could see that the display showing the remaining battery level was reading at only 50 per cent, meaning that not only would it soon begin slowing down but also that it wouldn't make it to the halfway point at 13 miles where we had pre-arranged to meet Matt for a fresh set.

I hadn't factored in the impact that the lower voltage in the States would have on the charging time for the wheelchair and so the six hours it had been on charge the previous evening had not been enough.

As difficult as it was to talk whilst driving, I did my best to convey to Chris the hopelessness of our situation.

But he told me to get my head down and concentrate, dropped back from running beside me and with mobile phone in hand, began planning the emergency rescue operation.

The theory was to move Matt to the 10-mile mark, but that would mean him having to run through the crowds with all the equipment on his back, or finding an alternative way of traversing New York.

My dream appeared to be slipping through my fingers. The wheelchair was slowing and by mile seven I was down to a walking pace and letting the team, who had trained so hard, down.

As I crawled around the streets of New York with two million pairs of eyes looking on, the weight of failure pressed heavily on my shoulders.

By this time I was now reliant upon my team to push the wheelchair, whilst I controlled its direction. I resolved to let them continue and leave me where the wheelchair came to a halt.

I ignored every one of their pleas otherwise and

headed to the side of the course, released the chin control and came to a stop.

I wasn't giving up, simply relinquishing the others from their responsibility for me, but they had totally bought into the 'all for one, one for all' principle and wouldn't hear of it.

As we got moving again, I must have had a face like thunder as I was overtaken by all and sundry. But the support and encouragement of the New York locals was nothing short of incredible. They just wouldn't let me wallow in self pity or give in.

In those moments, I learned one very special lesson: in life, whatever obstacle you are facing, you are stronger, and ultimately more likely to succeed if you allow yourself to rely upon your support network.

With only the police patrol vehicles bringing up the rear behind us, we met Matt for a Formula One style pit stop.

He had commandeered a rickshaw driver to take the thousands of pounds worth of equipment through the crowded streets in record time, including crossing an American football pitch whilst a match was in progress and doing likewise during a junior league game of baseball.

Mojo restored, I could not wait to get back up to speed and attack the rest of the course and we made our way through the field as we neared Central Park.

Reaching mile 22 and its gates, the combined effects of tiredness, concentration and the prolonged exposure to the November cold had taken its toll.

I was destroyed, both mentally and physically, struggling to hold my head upright and with each bump in the road I rode over, my neck screamed for me to stop.

I'd hit my own personal wall and it took a Herculean effort to continue.

My eyes were glazing over and I could feel myself slipping into the hazy world between consciousness and unconsciousness.

My body temperature had dropped to a dangerously low 34.2°C, rendering me almost hypothermic, and my control of the wheelchair was affected badly.

It must have been an incredible effort for the team to ensure my safety and that of the other runners, as my driving became more erratic.

I have very little recollection of how I managed to negotiate the turns and undulations through Central Park as we neared the finish line but, as we passed the 26 mile marker and embarked upon the final 385 yards, the surge of support coming from spectators, who had waited some seven hours for the final runners, appeared to pull me across the line.

And so it was that, with mum and dad behind me and my brothers waiting up ahead, our team of XIII true Heroes crossed the finish line.

It was not only a world first but a landmark moment.

In hospital, my disability defined who I thought I would become. A different person, confined by the constraints imposed by living in a body completely disassociated from my brain.

But overcoming this challenge proved that any such barrier did not exist in reality and crossing the finish line of the 2007 ING New York Marathon meant that I was still the same Matthew King I had always been.

19.

Paying Back

IT was only because of the strength and resolve I took from my family and friends that I managed to safely navigate the precarious line between survival and failure.

My story could so easily have been different. Take the case of Jon, who was in the bed in the corner of my bay in St Georges Ward in Stoke Mandeville.

Jon had been injured weeks before me whilst serving in the Army in Afghanistan. The Jeep in which he was travelling had rolled, leaving him paralysed from the neck down.

I'm not sure whether it was the age difference between us but we never really struck up too much of a bond. My main memory of him is seeing the light glowing from his computer screen deep into the night as he wiled away the hours watching films.

In all the months that I spent with Jon, I never once saw him receive a visitor of any kind.

I had almost taken it for granted that everybody had the same network of love and support behind them as I did but as the time passed, with Jon sitting in his wheelchair in the corner of the ward with little to no company, it struck me just how difficult his lonely journey must have been.

The trip to Sweden, in particular, changed my outlook and gave me the confidence that not only could I succeed myself, but I could help others and, maybe, make their journey just that little bit easier.

On returning, I threw myself into mentoring courses with the Backup Trust to give me the best foundation from which to work from when speaking to individuals suffering the darkest of times.

All I felt I could offer was honesty and, should anybody need it, proof that the apparently empty clichés constantly being thrown in their direction actually had truth as their foundation.

I initially asked Backup to only pair me with those who had suffered a similarly high level of spinal cord injury as mine that required ventilation and when I was asked to meet Joseph, was extremely nervous. To complicate matters further, he was 11 years old and autistic.

Entering the spinal unit in the Royal National Orthopaedic Hospital, Stanmore, I truly didn't know what my first words were going to be and very quickly after we were introduced, it dawned on me that these were going to be tough minutes.

Joseph was distant and completely dismissive of every one of my attempts to break the ice and get inside the barrier he had put up to the outside world.

I was out of my depth and didn't know what I could say to inspire him.

I did my best to relate to his hard times and show that life does continue, that he could go back to school, that skiing was possible, that life can be good again.

But for as much as I was trying to engage with him, it was a one-way conversation up until Joseph looked me in the eye and simply said, 'Please stop trying to motivate me.'

What he needed was the love and support of his family, and not some outsider preaching of the virtues of staying strong.

Rather than having a positive impact, as I came away, I was sure I had done some damage and that prospect was just heartbreaking.

But Joseph was the exception. In the months and years which followed, my mentoring continued on an ad hoc, as-and-when-needed basis.

I couldn't commit myself as much as I would have liked, for as fulfilling as I found helping others on their own respective journeys, I still had my own life to lead.

Following graduation, my goal of one day becoming a solicitor required me to begin the Legal Practice Course, a two-year post-graduate study at university in preparation.

Given the choice to do the LPC on a full or part-time basis, I jumped at the latter. Since leaving hospital, I hadn't given myself chance to slow down and doing it that way would free up the time to explore who I had become as a person and what I wanted to do with my life outside of the law.

An advert from the Spinal Injuries Association fortuitously found its way into my e-mail inbox around that time. The SIA were looking to fill a volunteer role as a peer advisor at the Royal National Orthopaedic Hospital, Stanmore and I jumped at the chance.

04.04.04

I headed along to SIA House in Milton Keynes for the interview, the first formal one I had ever sat through and I didn't really know what to expect.

For the next 40 minutes, I did my best to embellish my virtues and explain my experiences and how they would benefit the role.

I started the following week.

Arriving at Stanmore, fully dressed in my SIA attire, I felt a huge sense of pride. I knew that in the years to follow I would meet hundreds of individuals going through what I have, experiencing the same nightmares, isolation and desolation about their future.

For the majority, the prolonged stint as an inpatient is a test of the very fabric of their soul.

And so for two years, aside from my university studies, I travelled down the A1 to be the regular face patients could speak to and confide in.

I wasn't there to provide hope or inspiration but rather just a listening ear, somebody understanding, who they could bounce their thoughts and emotions off. I knew from first-hand experience that sometimes it is the people closest to you that are the hardest to unburden yourself to.

Given the loneliness of hospital, I found that patients often just wanted some company, to talk about normal things that provided an escape from the claustrophobia.

For over a year of my time in Stanmore, every week I would visit Darren, a young chap who had suffered his injury years earlier but who had developed a severe pressure sore.

He had not been able to get out of bed for 10 months. A bed which had become his prison.

Remarkably, Darren was one of the most upbeat and positive people I have ever come across. He could look out of the window towards the hospital gardens and beyond and yet, despite having the outside world so close, it was always out of reach.

Little did I know it, but two years later I would face my own battle with a pressure sore which left me confined to my bed for six months. The devastation is unbearable.

Unlike some of the others I met, he never gave up.

With no formal training to prepare me, I can't begin to describe how it felt to be told face-to-face that they wanted to end their lives.

Again, all I offered was my honesty; about the hard, long road ahead of them, the rewards waiting in the outside world, if only they could hang on that long.

I had the privilege of meeting individuals of all backgrounds and I developed as a person, growing from a young boy drawing on the strength and resources of those around me, to a man able to help others in their time of need.

I continued volunteering for three years up until I began my training contract with Stewarts Law when I could no longer spare the time.

My association with Variety, the children's charity, had flourished ever since their life-changing intervention in 2004 when they funded my powered wheelchair.

They are truly incredible and whilst I soon hit the age of 18 and no longer fell within their remit, I have never forgotten what they did for me.

Funding wheelchairs is just one arm of their work and they have a huge impact on the lives of sick, disabled and disadvantaged children and their families.

In the small way I have been able, I have done my best to persuade potential donors of their virtues and benefits, and to highlight the invaluable work they do.

04.04.04

As their Wheelchair Ambassador, whether it is speaking at award ceremonies, business lunches or simply attending the handing over of a Sunshine coach, I hope I have been adequately able to convey the impact they have had on my life.

Whilst my injury involved an enormous amount of pain and suffering, it was also a catalyst that brought about long-term good.

The turbulent rebuilding process, as I sought to put the fragments of my life back together, coincided with the formation of the Rugby Football League Benevolent Fund.

At the moment I went into that tackle on 04.04.04 there was no safety blanket for any player to fall back onto should they suffer a life changing injury while undertaking the game.

All players know they are exposed to risk but, like the vast majority, I always thought it would happen to somebody else.

As I lay there on the pitch knowing my neck was broken, there was nothing provided by the sport for me or my family in the critical hours, days and weeks which were to follow.

Given the physical nature of the sport, it should have been a given that the organisation, which prides itself on family being one of its virtues, should have had some kind of practical support mechanism in place, but back then it didn't.

Running onto the pitch that day, the insurance policy deemed adequate by the Rugby Football League was capped at a maximum pay out of £50,000.

With my legal knowledge, the equivalent in compensation for an injury such as mine, suffered in everyday life, would be about 300 times as much.

Despite having received the phone call informing them of my accident, when arriving in Leeds – where the game has its headquarters – my parents had absolutely no network at the RFL to rely upon.

There was no-one they could speak to, no help to arrange where they might stay whilst I was in intensive care, how the incidentals which arose were to be dealt with. Nothing was in place.

Mum and dad were alone and it was a naive and irresponsible approach to the welfare of their players by a governing body.

What followed was an ad hoc provision of assistance which put out fires as and when they arose and little was done to rectify the situation until some five weeks after my accident.

The 2004 Challenge Cup Final was a turning point for the Rugby Football League.

A marquee event in the sporting calendar, it was quickly pinpointed by my family and friends as a major fundraising opportunity to help mitigate, in some small way, the utterly inadequate financial means I had been provided with and upon which I will have to rely on for the rest of my life.

Around 70 of my family, friends and teammates travelled to Cardiff armed with 150 buckets and wearing their 'Go for It Matt' T-shirts, making as much noise as possible and harassing, in the nicest possible way, many of the unsuspecting fans into parting with their coins.

Part-way through fate intervened, bringing those with the power within the RFL face-to-face with the ones in need of its help.

Having negotiated her way into the corporate

hospitality suites, my cousin Sarah found herself in a lift surrounded by the upper echelons of the RFL.

The then president, Gary Hetherington was accompanied by current CEO Nigel Wood, Tim Adams and MP David Hinchliffe.

Coming face-to-face with her, it clicked with them that the situation just wasn't right; players and families shouldn't be so exposed and left to fend for themselves.

Something had to be done, and in those brief moments in the lift, the embryo of a working Benevolent Fund was formed.

In the months that followed, the building blocks were put in place to ensure that others injured in the future, wouldn't have to face the same trauma and insecurities we had.

To their credit, the RFL directed significant resources into making the Benevolent Fund the force it needed to be.

The prestigious, black tie, annual President's Ball was resurrected with all profits ploughed back into the Fund.

From every ticket sold for the Challenge Cup Final and Super League Grand Final, one pound was donated.

But aside from those financial contributions, of equal relevance was the importance placed upon player welfare.

Tragedy should not have been its impetus but now the RFL Benevolent Fund is a great source of support, not only for myself, but for every player at no matter what level, who has had their life turned upside down having taken the field.

From funding my university fees to paying for specialist adaptations to my wheelchair accessible vehicle, the Benevolent Fund has been a constant source of financial support.

The Rugby Football League is not the faceless organisation it felt like at the start. It is full of people with compassion and sincerity.

Richard Lewis was the RFL's chief executive at the time of my accident.

Without any obligation to do so, he spent many an hour on the motorway driving to visit my family and I to make sure he and the organisation he represented was doing all they could.

I'm certain that off the back of our meetings, and those he had with my parents, Richard made sure that much change for good came about.

In the first years of the Benevolent Fund, Dave Phillips was a constant source of support. He was the go-to individual within the Fund and was pivotal in funding state-of-the-art ventilators for me.

Latterly, Steve Ball has taken over this mantle. I have come to know him as an exceptional individual who only has the best interests of others at heart.

During the long years it has taken to get to this point and reflect upon my experiences, Steve has been a constant ally.

Not just through his position as general manager of the Fund but, more importantly, as a friend.

The same can be said of Tim Adams. He acted as chairman of the Benevolent Fund from 2006 and has been instrumental in its growth since its inception.

The expansion of the remit of the Benevolent Fund ran alongside that of XIII Heroes and having such friends to fall back on made the difference between me merely existing, and thriving.

Painting became a way I could offer some support

back. Every year since 2007 I have created a winter scene which has been reproduced on official Christmas cards sent out by the RFL and available for general purchase, the proceeds from which have been ploughed into helping others.

With my life becoming increasingly fulfilled, there was more to come. Opening my e-mail on 8 December, 2011 there was one from the Olympic organising committee.

My eyes scanned only the opening paragraph before I nearly burst. It read:

> 'We are delighted to give you a conditional offer to be one of just 8000 Torchbearers who will carry the Olympic Flame during the London 2012 Olympic Torch Relay.'

A mixture of excitement, pride and astonishment overwhelmed me and I picked up the phone to my grandad.

Months earlier, he had mentioned that he had submitted an application on my behalf and now I would play a part in the 2012 London Olympic Games.

The gradually increasing stream of e-mails from the organising committee only heightened my sense of anticipation as I counted down the days until 9 July, especially as the public's enthusiasm for the Games and the relay took hold.

My designated slot was to negotiate the 300 metres at 7:55am through Dunstable High Street and arriving at the Town Hall early on the day, through the gathering throng, my first task was to find a suitable way of attaching the Torch to the wheelchair.

Whilst working with the Olympic committee

organisers to finalise the adaptation, there were some tense minutes before they were satisfied that the torch was secure and I happy that the flame wouldn't be too close to my head when lit.

Dropped off at our relay points, the crowds gathered and so began the most incredible 60 minutes. As the bus stopped, one of the organisers stood up and clasped the torch nearest to me.

Stopping just short, he placed it in front of my face and slowly revolved it in his hands. I could see every detail; the 2012 London Olympic Games emblem, the 8,000 holes cut in it to represent each person on the relay and the beautiful detailing around the top where the flame would burn from.

With it mounted on my wheelchair, the bus doors opened, a wall of noise flooded in, and for the next 20 minutes or so I was at the centre of thousands of photos as everybody grasped the opportunity to picture the torch.

As the flame neared, the noise of the crowd went from a low murmur to a roar of cheers and encouragement.

There was only one problem, the kissing of the torches at transfer needed each to be held at 45 degrees so that the gas would ignite between them.

One of the organisers played my role in the ceremony. As the torches kissed, the flame erupted and with the nation watching, it was placed back on my wheelchair and the official photographs taken.

I swung the chin control back in front of my face, pushed upwards on the joystick and began my part in the nationwide relay.

Immediately I could feel heat. Intense heat.

I wanted to embrace the euphoric moment and to say I was honoured and proud is an understatement. Despite the uproar and pleas of the organisers to move quicker, I did my best to milk the moment.

I was able to see the smiles on people's faces, hear their shouts of support and see many of my friends legging it through the crowds to my left and right to get as many photographs of the flame as they could as I moved along the road.

But all too soon I could see the next relay runner waiting up ahead of me.

Pushing the chin control forward as far as it would go, the chair sped up and I moved away from the escorts running either side of me.

Their pleas for me to slow down fell on deaf ears, however. With open tarmac ahead of me, I swung the wheelchair towards the left-hand side of the road and immediately turned to my right, putting it into a spin.

It was a textbook execution of a 'doughnut', the wheelchair spinning quicker and quicker upon itself until I found myself pirouetting on the spot.

With the flame following the chair's every movement, I'm not sure whether the crowd were surprised, impressed or concerned that I was dangerously out of control.

20.

Tax Payer

MY career with Stewarts Law had rather fortuitous beginnings.

My studies at university led me into the law clinic, an optional module providing free legal advice to the public, thereby preparing me for my future career as a solicitor.

With my understanding of the problems faced by those having suffered spinal cord injuries, it was a natural avenue on which to try and give pertinent advice on their rights.

I'd planned that it would be an extension of the voluntary work that I was already doing at the Royal National Orthopaedic Hospital, Stanmore.

The fly in my ointment was that a firm was already in situ, offering such advice. Stewarts Law had been undertaking it for a good while and whilst that scuppered my plans, it identified a door I needed to be knocking on.

With a little research, I found out who headed up their pro bono service at Stanmore and in the weeks that followed pressed him into meeting me during one of his follow-up visits to the Unit.

As a result of it going well, I was offered a week-long work experience placement with them in the summer of 2007.

Travelling into London, it was my first time on a train since my accident. Inexplicably, I felt a huge sense of pride, it was a great feeling to be surrounded by others going to work.

Rush hour meant there wasn't room to swing a cat in the carriage, let alone allow my powered wheelchair, portable ramps, medical bags and support workers to enter with any sort of dignity. But there was nothing else for it, I was getting on that train!

Arriving at King's Cross, it became apparent that I was too tall to fit in the traditional black cabs that were parked in a long queue outside the station.

After half an hour I found one of the newer versions but I had to recline at 45 degrees to lower my head sufficiently to get it through the door. It was hardly the ideal way to arrive at the salubrious office in Lincoln's Inn Fields.

Passing through those prestigious doors signalled the start of three years' work experience with the firm. With each passing year, the nature of the work I was given became more demanding and testing and although overwhelming at first, I thrived on the challenges.

During that time, the firm moved to a state-of-the-art, ultra-modern set of offices just off Fleet Street in the City of London which brought with it a whole new level of accessibility and comfort for me.

With a job offer made, I was to start my Training Contract with Stewarts Law in October 2011.

I was 23, on the verge of a career as a lawyer in the City and had long ceased to be limited by the daily challenges of living with my injury.

The only drawback was the trials and tribulations it took to get from home in Langford to the capital.

It was time for me to take the next step, move out of the family home and begin living independently.

With only half of the stations equipped with lifts, getting to work on the underground was simply not an option. But travelling on the overground to City Thameslink from Bedford, coupled with a five-minute walk, was do-able.

After months of searching, it became obvious that buying the kind of property I needed wasn't feasible. They were too specialist, rarely came on the market and were outside my price range.

As a last resort, I began researching local housing associations. One of them responsible for much of the social housing in and around the Bedford area told me about Wixams, a new development being built in the outskirts.

I submitted an application form on a Monday and just days later, my phone rang. It was the association and they had identified a suitable property for me, should I want it.

I definitely did and, six months later, found myself crossing the threshold of my own beautiful bungalow. It suited my needs in every way with three bedrooms, a wet room – which I could now take a shower in for the first time in six years – large garden and ample parking, I could not have designed it better if I'd tried.

I moved in on a cold and snowy day in December 2010 and it was incredibly daunting to release the bonds of my support network. It was the opening of a new chapter in my life.

04.04.04

Although I was prepared to do four days a week, and thought I could, Stewarts were aware of the medical and logistical battles I would face on a daily basis, and insisted I work part-time for three days.

Any and all equipment which would allow me to perform my role as independently as possible would be provided and, as at school and university, I would have a scribe to assist with all the physical elements of the job.

With Pam agreeing to work with me for the duration of my training contract, everything was in place. All I had to do now was pass the LPC, which I did, earning a Distinction.

My working life in earnest, though, had a sartorially inelegant debut despite my routine beginning at 5.30am for a 10 o'clock start.

With support workers not wearing ties, and never having tied a knot before, I was reduced to having to describe it with my mouth and my eyes. That failed miserably, and to compound matters, I had the worst hair day.

Reliant upon one with a shaved head to style my hair was a huge failure.

In his not so delicate manner, he scooped up a handful of gel and proceeded to slap it, in one big lump, on the top of my head leaving me looking like a cross between Doc Brown from *Back to the Future* and Jedward.

I was the only one on the train as it pulled out of Bedford station and, having fallen asleep immediately, by the time I awoke at King's Cross, it was commuter-full and I was pinned in my space next to the toilet.

Waking up brought with it the unforeseen issue of my lowered eye level being directly in line with every backside from South East England, and with every jerk of the train, I was at risk of being smothered.

Exiting the station onto Fleet Street, rush-hour had died down, but finding myself amongst the hustle and bustle of London as I made my way into the offices of Stewarts Law, on my first day of bone-fide employment, I realised just how far – literally and metaphorically – I had come.

21.
Royal Appointment

IT was a normal day coming in from work on 25 April 2012. I gathered the post, tossed it to one side expecting the usual bills and junk mail and drove into the bedroom.

Stopping next at the suction machine, I spent 15 minutes performing chest physio, cough assists and suctions to keep my lungs healthy after a long day in the office.

Going back to the pile, one envelope stood out. It was addressed to Mr M. King Esq, and emblazoned with 'On Her Majesty's Service'.

Opening it, my world stopped as I read:

'The Prime Minister has asked me to inform you…'

Very quickly, confusion turned to euphoria as I read on:

'He is recommending that Her Majesty may be graciously pleased to approve that you be appointed an Officer of the Order of the British Empire in the Birthday 2012 Honours List.'

I didn't fully understand what it meant but knew that

this was something which happened to other people. I genuinely could not believe that I had done anything to deserve it.

Instinctively, the first thing I wanted to do was share the moment and seconds later I was on the phone to mum.

I told her about the letter and began reading it but 'The Prime Minister...' were the only words that came out of my mouth before she broke down in tears of joy.

'No, no, no... Oh Matthew, you deserve this,' she said through her sobs and in those words were reflected every moment of tragedy, desperation, hope and joy which we had endured and shared since 04.04.04.

But this was just March and with the Queen's Birthday Honours List announced in June, the weeks which followed were a trial of discipline as I remained silent.

As I lay in bed watching *Sky News* at 00:00 on 16 June, the release valve was finally opened. With the names of those receiving Honours scrolling across the bottom of the screen, mine surfaced on the list of sporting individuals recognised – 'Matt King, injured playing rugby league, has received an OBE for services to charity and those with disabilities' it read.

The influx of phone calls, text messages and e-mails received the following morning was astonishing.

In the days that followed, life quickly got back to normal and all there was to do was wait for the invitation to attend the investiture ceremony which would either be undertaken by the Queen, Prince Charles or Princess Anne.

Finally, the confirmation I was waiting for dropped through the letterbox in November saying, '*I am commanded to inform you that an Investiture will be held at Buckingham Palace on Friday, 25th January 2013, at which your attendance is requested.*'

It also said that Prince Charles would be conducting the ceremony.

Now it was time to get excited but with the invitation stating that recipients could only bring two family guests with them, this left me with a problem. Needing a support worker, that left little room for my family.

I contacted the Central Chancery at St James's Palace and, thankfully, after a lot of negotiation, four other tickets were provided for mum, dad, Andrew and Michael.

Wardrobe decisions were made and remade and we planned a 6.30am start for a 10 o'clock arrival at the Palace, leaving us plenty of time.

The first sign of trouble was when Ransford, the support worker travelling with us on the day, arrived 15 minutes late because he'd overslept.

Just minutes later, as we arrived at Junction 13 of the M1, my heart sank as a seemingly never ending line of brake lights were stationary in all three lanes of the motorway.

As we hit London, the rush-hour traffic was heavy as we slowly edged our way towards the Mall, the tension in the now silent van rising.

The only thing in dad's power was to ignore the satellite navigation, head into the back streets and hope we could circumvent the clogged up traffic.

We would make a short-term gain but, all too quickly, find ourselves coming back to the same queues.

Arriving at the Palace with just minutes to spare, we pulled up at the back of the queue of cars waiting to pass through the strict security checks, when a policeman walked up to ours and knocked on the driver's side window.

I thought it might be to congratulate me, but he pointed out in a surly manner that the offside brake light wasn't working and that, on this occasion, he was prepared to overlook it. As dad raised the window, although I was 26, I knew I was still in for a bollocking.

We went through the gates, drove over the gravel and past the Queen's Guard protecting the entrance and finally entered the inner courtyard of the Palace.

There was grandeur, beauty and opulence everywhere but my abiding memory is of the cold and I couldn't wait to get inside.

I surveyed the four steps in front of me but, as if reading my mind, a Beefeater came up behind me and requested that I accompany him to the side entrance which catered for wheelchair users.

I found myself sitting inside Buckingham Palace.

Aside from the beautiful carpet I was leaving wheelchair tracks on, stunning paintings adorned the walls and beautiful ornaments rested on the side table next to me.

The Beefeater explained that the recipients of Honours should gather in the Picture Gallery, whilst all their guests should take their seats in the Ballroom in which the investiture would take place.

With my medical needs, heading into the Gallery on my own was not possible and having explained that to the Beefeater, he relented and allowed one person to accompany me. In truth, there was only one choice.

Minutes later, mum and I found ourselves inside, surrounded by paintings of enormous value and importance.

The other recipients around me were a great deal older and I knew they had all achieved incredible personal feats of heroism, endeavour, commitment or dedication in order to find themselves in this room. I, on the other hand, felt I had done none of that.

Ever since my eyes opened to the voice of a doctor in Leeds General Infirmary, I had only done what needed to be done.

As a 17-year-old boy at the time, I had no choice but to draw on the strength of my family, my friends and those kind individuals caring for me in hospital and slowly but surely take each tiny step towards an unknown future.

Along that long, turbulent path to recovery I had been selfish, stubborn, reluctant and terrified. Alone, I would not have made it.

It was only the love and support network I relied on which took me past each obstacle encountered, as my eyes opened every morning to the horrific hand I believed I had been dealt.

In the darkest of moments, you discover the essence of who you are and, with their ceaseless, selfless help, desolation was replaced with hope and I chose to survive.

I can barely express and never repay my gratitude.

And yet here I sat in Buckingham Palace, about to receive one of the greatest honours that can be bestowed on an individual born in the Commonwealth. I had truly come full circle.

With such thoughts racing through my mind, I was suddenly brought back to the present. The general buzz of conversation was interrupted by the Lord Chamberlain of the Royal Household, who, standing at the entrance to the Picture Gallery, directed everyone to come towards him as he gave the instructions as to what to expect, and how to act in the minutes which followed.

So as to avoid a mass stampede passing through the Ballroom, we were called through in groups of 10 and I was in the third as we lined up in order.

04.04.04

With the National Anthem played, we made our way across the room and as I turned to my left and saw my family watching on, I could see the pride in dad's eyes,

All the while a Royal Beefeater remained by my side and, as much as I was in awe of where I was and what was about to happen, as he probed me with questions about my past, my mind instinctively returned to a field in Halifax:

'Stay calm, you are going to be fine...'

'Concentrate on your breathing, slow it down...'

'Matt, look at me. Focus on my eyes. Matt. Milton. Calm down, help is coming.'

A broken neck. Life in a wheelchair, no life at all.

Suddenly, I found myself first in line staring at Prince Charles. As instructed, moving forward, I stopped with my left shoulder to the Lord Chamberlain.

Waiting there to be called, I heard words I never dreamt possible as I lay there, dying on that pitch, 3,218 days earlier.

'Matthew King, appointed an Officer of the Order of the British Empire for services to charity and those with disabilities'

Engaging the motors of the wheelchair, believing anything is possible, I moved forward knowing that 04.04.04 was now just a date in the life of Matthew King.

Afterword
Richard Lewis CBE

THE day Matt King's life changed forever, rugby league also changed, and for the better. The renowned family on which the sport prides itself came together as we always knew it would, always has done, always will.

But this was different. Not only did we think it was a tragedy, a much over-used word, but we also knew this young man and his family would need a huge amount of help.

It was the catalyst for the Rugby Football League Benevolent Fund, an opportunity for numerous people who really care to come together to do good, for rugby league and for human beings to be at their best.

What we did not know then was that Matt and his family are very special people. Or that Matt would go on to lead not only a very fulfilling life, but also become an inspiration, another much over-used word but which this time barely does justice to the reality.

04.04.04

Matt is a shining light to many people, myself included. It is amazing what human spirit is capable of; to be able to give so much to others when their needs seem so great.

I first met him at his family's home in Bedfordshire – a day I'll never forget. Several months after his accident (had I left it too long, was it too soon, is there a 'right' time to visit?), I expected it to be difficult, despite what people had told me in advance.

The reality was I came away uplifted. Not only that, but in possession of a gift. A very valuable and treasured gift.

Matt had spent his first day as a mouth painter. He showed me an example and it took my breath away. I thought it was brilliant. The painter, speaking with great difficulty through a ventilator, thought it was okay.

He wasn't very happy with his first two efforts and this was apparently his third. He showed me his first two, they were also brilliant, each a noticeable improvement on the previous one.

We chatted about many things, about the future, how much he loved sport and was looking forward to going to rugby league matches, all sorts, all of which were incredible given the context. Incredible to me that is, but not to Matt.

When it was time to leave, Matt gave me the painting that I had so admired. I loved it and I loved the gesture. I had it framed and it has been in my office ever since – at the RFL, at Sport England and now at Wimbledon.

I often show it to visitors and explain the story behind it, proud of what Matt has achieved since that day we first met. Thank you Matt and thank you for writing this book. I know you want it to help other people and I am sure it will. It is an inspiring story from a truly remarkable young man.

Richard Lewis, July 2015

If you can't fly, then run,
If you can't run, then walk,
If you can't walk, then crawl,
But whatever you do,
You have to keep moving forward
– Martin Luther King Jr.

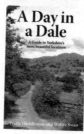

Be inspired.

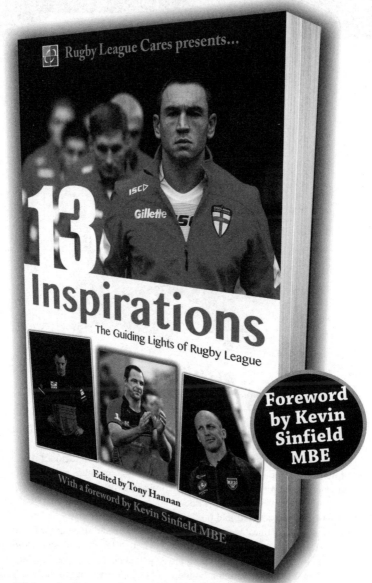

With contributions from many of the leading writers and
personalities in the game, **13 Inspirations** is a lively literary
collection in praise of the guiding lights of rugby league.

In aid of Rugby League Cares

Route 63: Around England on a Free Bus Pass

Dave Hadfield

Foreword by Sky Sports presenter Dave Clark

It was the first stage in an epic journey that would take him around the furthest flung corners of his native England, showing it to him from a completely new angle.

Already acclaimed for his books on sport and music, Hadfield broadens his canvas in his finest work yet.

Heading south along the Welsh Borders, west to Land's End, along the South Coast to Dover, through London and up the eastern side of the country to Newcastle, through the Pennines and the Lakes and back home to Lancashire; he chronicles what he sees and hears on an itinerary that involves over 100 local buses.

Better still, he does it all for nothing - on a bus pass for which he was qualified by Parkinson's Disease.

Undeterred by that disability, he explores the country he loves with a keen eye and fine ear for the absurd. Thoughtful and hilarious, *Route 63* will appeal to all who have enjoyed Hadfield's writing for the *Independent*, as well as his popular previous outings.

Those new to his unique style, can discover why he has been called Bolton's answer to Bill Bryson.

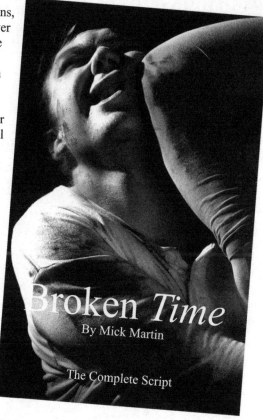

Investigate all our other titles and
stay up to date with our latest releases at
www.scratchingshedpublishing.co.uk